WHY DO SHEPHERDS NEED A BUSH?

WHY DO SHEPHERDS NEED A BUSH?

London's Underground History of Tube Station Names

DAVID HILLIAM

David Hilliam

25/06/11

First published 2010

The History Press
The Mill, Brimscombe Port
Stroud, Gloucestershire, GL5 2QG
www.thehistorypress.co.uk

British Library Cataloguing in Publication Data.
A catalogue record for this book is available from the British Library.

ISBN 978 0 7524 5526 6

Typesetting and origination by The History Press
Printed in Great Britain
Manufacturing managed by Jellyfish Print Solutions Ltd

CONTENTS

INTRODUCTION

The names of the 300 or so London Underground stations are so familiar to us as we strap-hang our way across the capital that we take them utterly for granted. We hardly ever question their meanings or origins – yet these well-known names are almost always linked with fascinating stories of bygone times.

Until the mid-nineteenth century, London was unbelievably rural, with names belonging to a countryside that we would neither recognise nor could imagine today. The old fields and turnpikes, market gardens and trees and bushes have completely disappeared, but their names still remain – given extra permanence as they are now forever enshrined as parts of our Underground network.

But who, in the twenty-first century, thinks of a real flesh and blood shepherd lolling back on a specially trimmed hawthorn bush, when travelling through Shepherd's Bush Underground Station? Who nowadays thinks of the original gigantic Fairlop Oak at the far end of the Central Line? And who, travelling through Totteridge and Whetstone on the Northern Line, imagines medieval soldiers sharpening their swords and daggers at the aptly named Whetstone just before engaging in the appallingly bloody battle of Barnet?

What about all those fifth- and sixth-century Saxon chieftains all bringing their families and followers to settle into what was dangerous new territory for them on a foreign island? Padda and Tota, Brihtsige and Wemba – none of them have any memorial, except that we unconsciously use their names as we speak of Paddington, Tottenham, Brixton and Wembley.

This book is not about the Underground itself, but about the names to be found on the network lines. It is hoped that both hardened old commuters and fresh-eyed new visitors to London will find this collection of origins an intriguing pathway into the rich, half-hidden history of England's capital…

… and as an extra, the second part of this book contains a short selection of other well-known London place-names with particularly interesting derivations.

David Hilliam

A BRIEF TIMELINE

The history of the various London Underground lines is complicated, as they were gradually formed bit by bit through the amalgamation of different railway companies. However, here is a much-abbreviated timeline.

1863	9 January	Metropolitan Line opens: Paddington to Farringdon
1864	13 June	Hammersmith and City Line opens
1868	1 October	District Line opens: High Street Kensington to Gloucester Road
1884	6 October	Circle Line completed
1890	November	Northern Line opens
1898	11 July	Waterloo and City Line opens
1900	27 June	Central Line opens
1906	10 March	Bakerloo Line opens
1906	15 December	Piccadilly Line opens
1969	7 March	Victoria Line officially opened: Warren Street to Victoria

[*Drawing by W. Newman.*]
A PROPHETIC VIEW OF THE SUBTERRANEAN RAILWAYS.

A cartoon in *Punch*, 26 September 1846, when the London underground
railway was first proposed. The very idea was considered to be ludicrous.

1979	**1 May**	Jubilee Line opens
1987	**31 August**	Docklands Light Railway opens: Tower Gateway and Stratford to Island Gardens

ACKNOWLEDGEMENTS

Most of the illustrations are taken from *Old and New London* by Walter Thornbury and Edward Walford, published in 1897 by Cassell and Company Ltd. The exceptions are: the cartoon 'A Prophetic View of the Subterranean Railways', which appeared in *Punch* on 16 September 1846; the illustrations of Old Charing Cross, Swiss Cottage and the Fairlop Oak, which were taken from *London Stories* by 'John O' London'; and the drawing of the bull's head at Hornchurch, which was drawn by the author.

A–Z OF TUBE STATION NAMES

ACTON TOWN W3
District and Piccadilly
Originally opened on 1 July 1879 as MILL HILL PARK
Name changed to ACTON TOWN on 1 March 1910

'Acton' means 'farm among the oak-trees' – coming from two Saxon words: *ac*, 'oak-tree' and *tun*, 'farm' or 'settlement'. Most English place names beginning with 'Ac' derive from the once plentiful crop of oak trees that grew there. There are over twenty other 'Acton' place names in the British Isles.

ALDGATE EC3
Circle and Metropolitan
Opened on 18 November 1876

'Old Gate'. One of the six gates built by the Romans in London's city wall. From here the road from London led to the Roman capital of Britain – Colchester. The gate was already old when the Saxons came here in the fifth century, so they called it Ealdgate. Pulled down in 1761, its name still lives on as an Underground station.

The original Aldgate, demolished in 1761.

ALDGATE EAST E1
Hammersmith & City, District
Opened on 6 October 1884
Re-sited on 31 October 1938

Obviously the name is borrowed from Aldgate, the Underground
station that had been opened eight years earlier. It had been proposed
to call it Commercial Road, but in the end the name Aldgate East
won the day, despite the fact that it is not sited particularly close to
the original London gate. See ALDGATE.

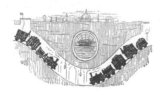

ALDWYCH WC2
A 'lost' station on the Piccadilly Line
Opened as STRAND on 30 November 1907
Name changed to ALDWYCH on 9 May 1915
Closed on 30 September 1994

Old Underground maps show Aldwych at the end of a branch-line from Holborn. Although now no longer in use, the name is too interesting to forget. When the Saxon King Alfred (871–899) defeated the invading Danes, he generously allowed some of them to live on in this area, under his rule. At that time it was well outside the city walls.

This Danish settlement was known by the Saxons as *Aldwic* – the 'old village' and the Church of St Clement Danes is said to be on the site of the old Danish burial ground. Drury Lane was known as *Via de Aldwych* in the Middle Ages, and the name was revived when this part of London, together with an Underground station, was modernised in the early twentieth century.

Sadly, Aldwych Underground Station was closed on 30 September 1994. It is one of more than forty London Underground stations that have closed or been re-sited over the years.

ALL SAINTS E14
Docklands
Opened on 31 August 1987

Named after All Saints' church in East India Dock Road, which was built in the years 1821–23. The parish of Poplar was created in 1821 and the parishioners raised over £30,000 – a very considerable sum in those days – to build their parish church. Designed by Charles Hollis, the church was consecrated in 1823.

ALPERTON MIDDLESEX
Piccadilly
Opened as PERIVALE-ALPERTON on 28 June 1903
Name changed to ALPERTON on 7 October 1910

The name comes from a Saxon chief named Ealhbeart. It is Ealhbeart's *tun*, or 'settlement'.

AMERSHAM BUCKINGHAMSHIRE
The terminus of the Metropolitan Line
Opened on 1 September 1892

Named after a Saxon landowner called Ealgmund. It is Ealgmund's
ham, or 'homestead'.

ANGEL N1
Northern
Opened on 17 November 1901

The Angel was, for centuries, one of the most important inns in
England, as it was the nearest staging post to London on the Great
North Road (nowadays upstaged by the M1 motorway). The Angel
was mentioned by Charles Dickens in *Oliver Twist* and it remained
an inn until 1899. It later became a Lyons' Corner House. The site
has now been taken over by a bank. The Underground station serves
to remind us of the famous inn that once stood here.

ARCHWAY N19
Northern
Opened as HIGHGATE on 22 June 1907
Name changed to ARCHWAY (HIGHGATE) on 11 June 1939
Name changed to HIGHGATE (ARCHWAY) on 19 January 1941
Changed finally to ARCHWAY in December 1947

The Underground station and the North London district of
Archway take their name from Archway Road, first built in 1813
with an impressive viaduct designed by John Nash (1752–1835)
in the style of a Roman aqueduct, 36 feet high (11 metres) and
18 feet wide (5.48 metres). The present viaduct used by the road was
designed and built in 1897 by Sir Alexander Binnie (1839–1917).

Archway is near the spot where Dick Whittington famously heard
the bells of London telling him to 'Turn again, Whittington … thrice
Mayor of London!'

ARNOS GROVE N14
Piccadilly
Opened on 19 September 1932

Arnos Grove was the former name of a large country house built
on the site of a medieval religious house known as Arnholt Wood in
the fourteenth century. It is now a beautiful retirement home called
Southgate Beaumont – but its original name is preserved in the name
of the Underground station, opened in 1932.

ARSENAL N5
Piccadilly
Opened as GILLESPIE ROAD on 15 December 1906
Name changed to ARSENAL (HIGHBURY HILL) on 31 October 1932
Use of HIGHBURY HILL gradually dropped over the years

Arsenal Football Club was founded in 1886, with its first football ground
in Woolwich. Arsenal Underground Station is named after this ground.
However, Arsenal Football Club moved to its Highbury Stadium in 1913.

There was an establishment here for making and testing arms
dating from Tudor times, and was granted the title Royal Arsenal by
George III in 1805. During the Second World War it employed 40,000
workers making armaments. However, Royal Arsenal ceased to be a
military establishment in 1994 and has now been developed for housing.

BAKER STREET NW1
Bakerloo, Circle, Hammersmith & City, Jubilee and
Metropolitan
Opened on 10 January 1863

Baker Street itself is not named after any bread maker. The Baker
after whom the street is named was William Baker, a builder in the
mid-eighteenth century who originally laid out the road. Opened
on 10 January 1863, this station saw the first underground journey
in the world.

Within walking distance: London Planetarium
                             Madame Tussaud's

Regent's Park
Royal Academy of Music
London Zoo

SHERLOCK HOLMES IN BAKER STREET

Baker Street is famous throughout the English-speaking world as the street where the detective Sherlock Holmes lived.

The house on which Sir Arthur Conan Doyle based his fiction was actually No. 21, the home of his friend Dr Malcolm Morris. In 1866 Conan Doyle thoroughly examined the house and based his 'No. 221A' on it. He made one alteration, however, to disguise it from the prying public: he gave his imaginary house only two front windows instead of three.

221B Baker Street is now the Sherlock Holmes Museum.

BALHAM SW12
Northern
Opened on 6 December 1926

The name Balham was first recorded in AD 957 as Bælgenham – which possibly meant that it was a 'smooth or rounded enclosure'. A more likely explanation is that it was the *ham*, or 'homestead', of a Saxon chief named Bealga.

BANK EC2
Central, Docklands, Northern, Waterloo & City
Waterloo & City opened as CITY on 8 August 1898
Northern Line opened as BANK on 25 February 1900
Central Line opened as BANK on 30 July 1900
Waterloo & City renamed BANK on 26 October 1940
Docklands Line opened as BANK on 29 July 1991

Bank gets its name because it is so near the Bank of England, founded in 1694. The actual Bank of England building however, designed by Sir John Soane, dates from 1788.

The word 'bank' comes from the Italian word *banco*, meaning a 'bench' – this particular bench would have been that on which money changers would display their money.

Within walking distance: Bank of England Museum
Guildhall
Mansion House
Stock Exchange
Merchant Taylors' Hall
St Margaret Lothbury
St Stephen Walbrook

BARBICAN EC2
Circle, Hammersmith & City, Metropolitan
Opened as ALDERSGATE STREET on 23 December 1865
Name changed to ALDERSGATE & BARBICAN in 1923
Changed finally to BARBICAN on 1 December 1968

The development of this area since the Second World War, with the new Guildhall School of Music and Drama and its theatre and concert hall, has given the name Barbican a totally new meaning for Londoners. In fact, it's easy to forget just what a barbican originally was.

During the castle-building days of the Middle Ages, a 'barbican' was an outer fortification or watchtower outside the main walls. Here in London, the Barbican was some sort of extra defence work constructed outside the main wall. Unfortunately, we can't be certain what it looked like as it was pulled down by Henry III in 1267 after his civil war with the barons.

Aldersgate itself was one of the six gates in the city wall originally built by the Romans. The origin of the word 'barbican' is uncertain – but it has been suggested that it derives from an Arab or Persian term *barbar khanah*, meaning 'house on the wall'.

Within walking distance: Barbican Centre
Guildhall School of Music and Drama
London Wall
Museum of London
St Bartholomew the Great

BAKERLOO – A 'GUTTER TITLE'!

Hundreds of thousands of people travel on the Bakerloo Line every day – and no one is in the least bothered about its name.

However, when the line first opened in 1906, many Londoners were quite disgusted by this brand new name, coined by the *Evening News*.

It was the first Underground line to run from north to south in London, linking Baker Street and Waterloo, so it seemed quite natural to invent this rather chirpy name for it.

However, in *The Railway Magazine*, an outraged reader called Bakerloo a 'gutter title' and complained that such a name 'is not what we expect from a railway company. English railway officers have more dignity than to act in this manner.'

What a horror! But then, this was Edwardian England!

BARKING ESSEX
Central   (see BARKINGSIDE)
Opened by the London, Tilbury & Southend Railway on 13 April 1854
First used by Underground trains on 2 June 1902

BARKINGSIDE ESSEX
District, Hammersmith & City
Opened by the Great Eastern Railway on 1 May 1903
First used by Underground trains on 31 May 1948

'Berica's people'. Like so many English place names, Barking comes from the name of a Saxon leader – in this case, Berica – who came here and settled with his family and friends. The Old Saxon word *ingas* meant 'family' or 'followers', so place names containing 'ing' almost always point to a Saxon chief and his group of followers. Other examples include Tooting, Paddington and Kensington.

BARONS COURT W14
District, Piccadilly
Opened on 9 October 1905

This is not an ancient name. In fact it was invented in the late nineteenth century by Sir William Palliser for his housing development to the west of North End Road. He probably intended it as a sort of companion piece to the name Earls Court, but there is no connection between the two. As with so many place names, it became firmly established when it was adopted by the Underground system as a station name.

BAYSWATER W2
Circle, District
Opened on 1 October 1868

Bayswater has a fascinating derivation. According to an old medieval legend, Charlemagne (747–814), the great king of the Franks, gave a magical horse to four brothers. When only one of these brothers

The Bayswater Conduit in 1798: 'a watering-place for horses'.

was mounted, the horse was of normal size, but if all four brothers mounted it, the horse would miraculously lengthen itself to seat them all!

The name of this extraordinary steed was Bayard, and the story was so famous throughout Europe in medieval times that the very name Bayard came to mean a horse.

It seems a far cry from Charlemagne to Bayswater, but in fact the name Bayswater is derived from a drinking place for horses – a 'Bayards' Watering'.

The point is that there are natural springs nearby, which once provided refreshment for many generations of 'bayards'.

BECKTON E6
BECKTON PARK E6
Docklands
Both stations opened on 28 March 1994

So many London names are derived from Saxon chieftains that it may come as a surprise to learn that the district known as Beckton comes from the name of a nineteenth-century producer of coal gas – Simon Adams Beck. He was the governor of the Gas Light and Coke Co., which bought a site in East Ham and was particularly successful in bringing the benefits of cheap gas lighting to London.

BECONTREE ESSEX
District
Opened as GALE STREET by the London Midland & Scottish Railway on
*   28 June 1926*
Name changed to BECONTREE on 18 July 1932
First used by Underground trains on 12 September 1932

'Beohha's tree'. In early Saxon times, trees were often used as landmarks for meetings and assemblies. The Saxon chief Beohha must have used this easily recognisable tree to serve as a rallying point.

Belsize House in 1800, demolished in 1854.

BELSIZE PARK NW3
Northern
Opened on 22 June 1907

The name is a reminder of Belsize Manor, an important manor house that existed in one form or another from the fourteenth century until it was pulled down in 1854.

The house and grounds were large and beautiful – Samuel Pepys thought the gardens were the most noble he had ever seen. Its very name – Belsize – came from two Norman French words: *bel assis*, meaning 'beautifully situated'.

BERMONDSEY SE1
Jubilee
Opened on 17 September 1999

'Beormund's island'. This isn't really an island, but the name refers to an original Saxon settlement here on slightly higher land among the watery marshes. Beormund was the Saxon chief who lived here with his followers.

BETHNAL GREEN E1
Central
Opened on 4 December 1946

Bethnal is another Saxon name. The second part of the word means 'corner', but it is not known whether the first part refers to a stream or a person. 'Bethnal' could have meant a corner or bend in a river, or else a 'place where Blytha lives'.

Within walking distance: Victoria & Albert Museum of
                                Childhood

THE BLITZ AND 'BOMBERS' MOONS'

During the Blitz in the Second World War, seventy-nine Underground stations were used regularly as air-raid shelters. It has been estimated that 177,000 people used them. The Liverpool Street extension had not been completed at that time, so no trains were running along that stretch of line under the East End. The result was that many people literally lived there for weeks at a time.

The parts of London worst affected by the Blitz were Holborn, the City, Westminster, Shoreditch, Southwark and Stepney. The Thames was a perfect navigation aid for the German bombers, especially when there was a full moon. Londoners came to call these 'bombers' moons'.

BLACKFRIARS SE1
Circle, District
Opened on 30 May 1870

In 1221 a monastery was founded in Chancery Lane for Dominican monks. Dominicans, by tradition, always wore black habits, so the monastery became known for its 'black friars'.

The monastery was closed down in 1538 by Henry VIII, but it had been a place of great importance. Parliaments had met there, and a court sitting there heard the divorce case against Catherine of Aragon, Henry VIII's first wife.

The black-robed monks are remembered in the names of Blackfriars Road, Blackfriars Bridge and other places in this area. The only piece of the original monastery left today is a part of a wall in Ireland Yard. In 1613 William Shakespeare bought a house nearby for £140 – but did not live in it himself.

Within walking distance: Dr Johnson's House
                             St Bride's church

BLACKHORSE ROAD E17
Victoria
Opened on 1 September 1968

Blackhorse Road was built on Blackhorse Fields, and both road and fields took their name from the Blackhorse Inn in Evelyn Street. Black horses still feature in the attractive artwork decorating this station. Despite this, however, a conflicting fact exists – the Blackhorse Road was called Black House Lane in the early nineteenth century – so are the horses simply the result of mispronunciation? We will never know.

BLACKWALL E14
Docklands
Opened on 28 March 1994

The name Blackwall comes from the black artificial bank constructed here to enable building to take place along the marshy banks of the Thames. The area was used for making and repairing ships and was also a place of arrival and departure. The Virginia Settlers under Captain John Smith set off from here in 1606 to found the first permanent colony in America.

BOND STREET W1
Central, Jubilee
Opened on 24 September 1900

Sir Thomas Bond, a seventeenth-century speculator, developed this area when he bought the land in 1664, hence, Bond Street.

It quickly became a fashionable shopping area, and over the years many famous people have taken lodgings above the shops: Jonathan Swift, Edward Gibbon, William Pitt the Elder, Lawrence Sterne, James Boswell, Admiral Nelson and his mistress Lady Hamilton.

'Prinny' – the Prince of Wales who later became George IV – had a bet with Charles James Fox, the liberal statesman, as to how many cats they would see on either side of Bond Street as they took a stroll there. Fox easily won the bet – thirteen cats to none – as he had cunningly chosen the sunny side!

Within walking distance: The Wallace Collection

BOROUGH SE1
Northern
Opened on 18 December 1890

The borough here is the Borough of Southwark, famous for being the setting off point for Chaucer's Canterbury pilgrims.

The Tabard Inn, where the pilgrims gathered, is no longer here, but the site is now occupied by Talbot Yard, Borough High Street.

The importance of Borough High Street can easily be imagined, as it was once the main road to London Bridge from the south. As London Bridge was the *only* bridge across the Thames until 1750, every coach load of travellers had to come this way. Furthermore, as London Bridge itself was too narrow for coaches, Borough High Street became the inevitable terminus. It was a flourishing, bustling area, with vast numbers of inns and a pillory, which stood in the middle of the street until 1620.

Shakespeare would have known this area well, as the original Globe Theatre was nearby – and today the modern reconstructed Globe still pulls in the crowds.

BOSTON MANOR MIDDLESEX
Piccadilly
Opened as BOSTON ROAD on 1 May 1883
Name changed to BOSTON MANOR on 11 December 1911

Named after the beautiful Jacobean manor house, Boston Manor, built in 1623, which can now be visited free of charge, is 'one of West London's lesser-known gems'. The house is about half a mile (0.8 kilometres) from the Underground station. The name Boston itself was derived in this instance from Bordeston – the *tun*, or 'farm', of someone named Bords who lived here in the Middle Ages.

BOUNDS GREEN N11
Piccadilly
Opened on 19 September 1932

'A green area belonging to the family of le Bonde'. A John le Bonde is recorded as being the tenant in 1294. Remarkably, his name still flourishes here more than seven centuries later.

BOW CHURCH E3
Docklands   (see BOW ROAD)
Opened on 31 August 1987

Named after the local church, the full name of which is St Mary Bow Church.

BOW ROAD E3
District, Hammersmith & City
Opened on 11 June 1902

Queen Matilda (1080–1118), wife of Henry I and daughter of Malcolm, King of Scotland (he appears in Shakespeare's *Macbeth*), had an accident while fording the River Lea near here. She got herself 'well washed' and only just escaped drowning. Indeed, some of her attendants did lose their lives in the river.

To give thanks, and to avoid a repetition of the accident, she had a bridge built here. It was the first arched bridge in England, and was called a 'bow' bridge.

This in turn gave its name to the road leading to it – Bow Road – and also to the whole district, Stratford-le-Bow.

Bow Bridge – the first arched bridge in England.

BRENT CROSS NW4
Northern
Opened as BRENT on 19 November 1923
Name changed to BRENT CROSS on 20 July 1976

The name Brent is Celtic – that is, it goes back to prehistoric times
even before the Romans or Saxons came to England. The river Brent
has been thought to mean 'holy one'.

When this Underground station opened in 1923 it was named
simply Brent, but this was changed to Brent Cross in 1976, when the
nearby Brent Cross Shopping Centre was opened. 'Cross' refers to
the fact that it is the centre of three major trunk roads.

BRIXTON SW2
Victoria
Opened on 23 July 1971

In 1062, just before the Norman Conquest, this name was recorded
as Brixges stane – the stone of a Saxon chieftain called Brihtsige.
Such a stone would have been used as a landmark meeting place in
early Saxon times, like the tree in Becontree.

BROMLEY-BY-BOW E3
District, Hammersmith & City
Opened as BROMLEY by the London, Tilbury & Southend Railway on
*   31 March 1858*
First used by Underground trains on 2 June 1902
Name changed to BROMLEY-BY-BOW on 18 May 1968

'The wood near Bow where the broom or brambles grow'.
(See BOW ROAD)

BUCKHURST HILL ESSEX
Central
Opened by the Eastern Counties Railway on 22 August 1856
First used by Underground trains on 21 November 1948

'Buckhurst' derives from two Saxon words: *boc hyrst*, meaning 'beech grove'.

Interestingly, our word 'book' also comes from this Saxon word for a beech tree.

Even before books as we know them were invented, wooden writing tablets were made of thin slices of beech wood, on which letters known as runes could be scratched. These, of course, were pieces of *boc*.

BURNT OAK MIDDLESEX
Northern
Opened on 27 October 1924

The Romans used to mark boundaries by burning a conspicuous tree. Perhaps this name refers to some such noteworthy landmark – literally a burned oak tree, either branded deliberately or else struck by lightning. In Prehistoric and early Saxon times, trees and stones were used as meeting points. See BECONTREE, BRIXTON and FAIRLOP.

CALEDONIAN ROAD N1
Piccadilly
Opened on 15 December 1906

When the Caledonian Road was first built in 1826 it was known as Chalk Road, because of the chalky soil in that area. However, its name was changed to Caledonian Road after an orphanage, the Caledonian Asylum, was built there.

The orphanage was built specially for Scottish boys whose fathers had been killed on war service, or whose parents were too poor to look after them. In 1846 it took in girls as well as boys. The orphanage moved to Bushey, Hertfordshire, in 1903 and the building in Caledonian Road was demolished. However, the name for the road remained, and when the Underground station opened here in 1906, it seemed only natural to call it 'Caledonian Road'.

Caledonia was the ancient Roman name for Scotland, deriving from Caledones, the term for the inhabitants of north-west Scotland.

CAMDEN TOWN NW1
Northern
Opened on 22 June 1907

The name Camden Town has an extremely roundabout origin ultimately connected with the name of William Camden (1551–1623), a famous Elizabethan schoolmaster, historian and writer. However, Camden would have been astonished if he had been told that a large area to the north of London would bear his name long after his death. After all, this part of modern London was completely open countryside in his day – and in any case, he had no connection whatever with the area.

Camden had a house in Surrey, which was later bought by a family named Pratt. Much later, in 1765, a Charles Pratt became Attorney General and was created a baron. He decided to take the title Baron Camden – naming himself after his house, the former home of old William Camden. This Baron Camden was further ennobled to become an earl, becoming very rich and buying up many acres of fields in north London.

In 1791 Lord Camden decided to lease this land for the building of 1,400 new houses, and the newly built-up area became known as Camden Town.

The Underground station was opened here in 1907 – nearly three centuries after the death of the old schoolmaster, William Camden.

Within walking distance: London Zoo
                                     Regent's Park

CANADA WATER SE16
Jubilee, East London
Opened on 17 September 1999

The whole of the former docklands area has now been transformed. Canada Water is now a lake and wildlife refuge in Rotherhithe. The lake is named after Canada Dock, which used to be on this site and was principally used by ships importing and exporting goods from Canada.

CANARY WHARF E14
Docklands, Jubilee
Opened on 17 September 1999

Canary Wharf was built in 1936, largely for the importing of fruits and produce from the Canary Islands.

Interestingly, the Canary Islands themselves were named because of the large wild dogs that the ancient Romans found there – *canis* being the Latin word for 'dog'.

Word history has some curious twists – in this case from ancient dogs to a modern railway station!

CANNING TOWN E16
Docklands, Jubilee
Opened on 28 March 1999

This area of London was first developed in the early nineteenth century, and some believe that it was named in honour of Charles

John Canning (1812–62), an English statesman and first Viceroy of India. A more likely alternative suggestion however, is that it was named after a firm whose premises once stood in the area.

CANNON STREET EC4
Circle, District, Docklands
Opened by the South Eastern Railway on 1 September 1866
Underground station opened on 6 October 1884

It would be easy to imagine that Cannon Street and Cannon Street Station get their names in some way from military cannons. However, somewhat surprisingly, the word 'cannon' in these names is a reference to all the candle makers who used to live and work there. The present name is a corruption of the original Candlewick Street.

Within walking distance: St Stephen Walbrook

CANONS PARK MIDDLESEX
Jubilee
Opened as CANONS PARK (EDGWARE) on 10 December 1932
  (becoming simply CANONS PARK sometime in 1933)

The 'Canons' in this name derive from the fact that the Augustinian Canons of St Bartholomew's, Smithfield, held the land here back in the fourteenth century. The land came to be known as Canons – so when the 1st Duke of Chandos built a large country house here in the eighteenth century, he took up the name and called it Canons.

Unfortunately, his son, the 2nd Duke, had to demolish the house to pay off his enormous debts – nevertheless, the name Canons Park still clung to the grounds of the old house, and of course it was perpetuated even more firmly when the Underground station opened in 1932.

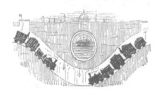

CHALFONT (CHALFONT & LATIMER) BUCKINGHAMSHIRE
Metropolitan
Opened as CHALFONT ROAD on 8 July 1889
Name changed to CHALFONT & LATIMER on November 1915

A tenth-century manuscript refers to this place as Caedeles funta, which means 'Caedel's spring or fountain'. By the time of the Domesday Book in 1086, this had turned to Celfunta, and this version gradually developed into the present Chalfont. (See LATIMER).

CHALK FARM NW3
Northern
Opened on 22 June 1907

There's nothing at all chalky about Chalk Farm! The name goes back to Saxon times, when it was known as Chaldecote, meaning 'cold cottages'!

Old Chalk Farm in 1720. It became a favourite spot where duels took place – often resulting in deaths.

In the seventeenth century there was an Upper Chalcot Farm in this area, and this form of the name is still perpetuated in Chalcot Crescent, Chalcot Gardens, Chalcot Road and Chalcot Square.

There was also a Lower Chalcot Farm, which became a tavern in the nineteenth century and was known as Chalk Farm Tavern. Chalk Farm then became firmly established when the Northern Line arrived here in 1907.

CHANCERY LANE WC2
Central (NB – closed on Sundays)
Opened on 30 July 1900

In the Middle Ages this lane was known as New Street, but in 1377 – in the time of Chaucer – the Keeper of the Rolls of Chancery was given his office here, and so the name changed to Chancellor's Lane. Successive Keepers of the Rolls of Chancery had their office here until 1896. The site is now occupied by the Maughan Library – the largest library of King's College London.

The very words 'chancery' and 'chancellor' have a curious and fascinating derivation. They come from the Latin word *cancelli* – the bars or rails that surrounded the Roman judgement seat. Curiously, in churches the word 'chancel' also comes from the same Latin word – and in churches the *cancelli* refers to the bars of the communion rail.

Within walking distance: The Charles Dickens Museum
                                                    Dr Johnson's House
                                                    Inns of Court and Temple

CHARING CROSS WC2
Bakerloo, Jubilee, Northern
Bakerloo Line opened as TRAFALGAR SQUARE on 10 March 1906
Northern Line opened as CHARING CROSS on 22 June 1907
After various other variant names, the combined stations opened as
  CHARING CROSS on 1 May 1979

The royal and romantic story behind this name goes back over 700 years to the year 1290. King Edward I (reigned 1272–1307) was just about to launch a savage attack on Scotland, and his queen,

The original thirteenth-century Charing Cross, which stood at the top of
Whitehall on the spot now taken by the statue of Charles I on horseback.

Eleanor of Castile, was travelling north to join him. However, on her journey north, she died quite unexpectedly in the little village of Harby in Nottinghamshire, aged only forty-six.

Edward was devastated, and immediately rushed back south – but alas, he could do nothing but make arrangements for her funeral.

Eleanor had to be taken back to Westminster in stages, and Edward ordered a beautiful memorial cross to be erected in each of the stopping places. In all, there were twelve: at Lincoln, Grantham, Stamford, Geddington, Northampton, Stony Stratford, Woburn, Dunstable, St Albans, Waltham, Cheapside, and – best known of all – the final village just before Westminster itself – Charing.

Inevitably, the village became known by the name of the memorial: Charing Cross.

Today, in the forecourt of Charing Cross Railway Station, surrounded by parked cars and taxis, there is a tall stone monument – a memorial to Eleanor – the 'Charing Cross'. Somewhat disappointingly it is a Victorian replacement of the original cross, which stood at the top of Whitehall on the site now occupied by the statue of Charles I on horseback.

Within walking distance: Cleopatra's Needle
                                  The National Gallery
                                  The National Portrait Gallery
                                  St Martin-in-the-Fields
                                  Savoy Hotel
                                  Strand
                                  Trafalgar Square

CHESHAM BUCKINGHAMSHIRE
Metropolitan
Opened on 8 July 1889

Chesham derives from the Old English word *ceaster*, 'a heap of stones', and *hamm*, 'a water meadow'. In the Domesday Book it is called Cestreham – a clearing or homestead near a pile of rubble.

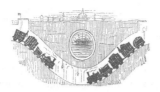

CHIGWELL ESSEX
Central
Opened by the Great Eastern Railway on 1 May 1903
First used by Underground trains on 21 November 1948

There are two possible derivations. Chigwell may be named after a Saxon called Cica or Cicca who once lived here by a well or spring.

Alternatively, Chigwell may be derived from the Old English word *ceacge*, meaning 'gorse', in which case the name means 'a well surrounded by gorse bushes'.

CHISWICK PARK W4
District
Opened as ACTON GREEN on 1 July 1879
Name changed to CHISWICK PARK & ACTON GREEN in March 1887
Finally changed simply to CHISWICK PARK on 1 March 1910

'Chiswick' means 'cheese farm'. The Old English word *wic* refers to a specialised farm, and was often linked to the name of the produce of that farm. Keswick in the Lake District is a variation of the same name, also indicating a cheese farm. Butterwick obviously produced butter; Smethwick had its smithy; and Gatwick, site of today's busy airport, had its goats.

CHORLEYWOOD HERTFORDSHIRE
Metropolitan
Opened as CHORLEYWOOD on 8 July 1889
Name changed to CHORLEYWOOD & CHENIES on 1 November 1915
Changed back to CHORLEYWOOD in 1934
Finally, the one-word version CHORLEYWOOD appeared c.1964

Chorley derives from two Saxon words: *ceorla*, 'peasants' and *leah*, 'woodland clearing' or 'glade'. 'Chorleywood' means 'clearing in the peasants' wood'.

A 'churl' (deriving from *ceorla*) is a forgotten word today, but it was formerly used to mean a free peasant or countryman. Although we have lost the word 'churl', we still retain the adjective 'churlish' to mean surly or ill mannered. Linguistically speaking then, the inhabitants of Chorleywood may be said to be churlish!

CLAPHAM COMMON E4
Northern
Opened on 3 June 1900

CLAPHAM NORTH E4
Northern
Opened as CLAPHAM ROAD on 3 June 1900
Name changed to CLAPHAM NORTH on 13 September 1926

CLAPHAM SOUTH E4
Northern
Opened on 13 September 1926

The Domesday Book spells Clapham as *Clopeham*, which means 'village or homestead on the hill'.

COCKFOSTERS HERTFORDSHIRE
Piccadilly
Opened on 31 July 1933

Cockfosters Station is the northern terminus of the Piccadilly Line, near the ancient and royal forest of Enfield Chase.

The Chief Forester of Enfield Chase had a house on the edge of this forest. It is now a hotel called West Lodge Park. However, before its present name, this house was known as Cockfosters – the home of the 'Cock' or 'Chief' Forester. The name could easily have been lost – but when the station was opened in 1933, it became firmly and permanently established.

A possible alternative explanation is that the word derives from the personal name of a family living in the area.

COLINDALE NW9
Northern
Opened on 18 August 1924

Colindale may well be derived from the name of the river Colne, and so it would mean the 'Colne dale' or 'valley'. However, an alternative explanation is that it may come from a family called Collin, who are known to have lived hereabouts in the sixteenth century.

COLLIERS WOOD SW19
Northern
Opened on 13 September 1924

'Woodland occupied by charcoal burners'. Charcoal used for fuel gave this area its name. Charcoal burners are known to have worked here in the sixteenth century.

COVENT GARDEN WC2
Piccadilly
Opened on 11 April 1907

This land was once the herb and vegetable garden belonging to the Convent of St Peter at Westminster – better known today as Westminster Abbey. This 'convent garden' supplied the monks with their vegetables, and surplus produce was sold off to the local inhabitants.

When the monasteries were destroyed by Henry VIII, the land passed to the Duke of Somerset, and then to John Russell, the 1st Earl of Bedford.

In 1631, the 4th Earl of Bedford began to create the square and develop the area. He commissioned Inigo Jones to design a new piazza and the Church of St Paul. Then, in 1670, the 5th Earl of Bedford

Covent Garden market in about 1820. St Paul's church is seen at the back of
the picture.

obtained a licence to hold a flower, fruit and vegetable market in
the square, thus continuing the tradition begun by the earlier
convent garden.

The square at Covent Garden has been compared with the
square at Leghorn in Italy and the Place des Vosges in Paris. It was
so popular that it became a town-planning trendsetter and inspired
the numerous other London squares which were laid out in
succeeding decades.

Within walking distance: Courtauld Institute Galleries
                              (Somerset House)
                              Covent Garden piazza
                              The Royal Opera House
                              St Paul's, Covent Garden (wall
                              tablets commemorating many actors)
                              London Transport Museum

CROSSHARBOUR E14
Docklands
Opened on 13 August 1987

This station is built in the right-angled cross formed by Millwall Inner Dock and the two docks at either end running at right-angles to it – the Main Section Dock and the Millwall Outer Dock

CROXLEY HERTFORDSHIRE
Metropolitan
Opened as CROXLEY GREEN on 2 November 1925
Name changed to CROXLEY on 23 May 1949

This name derives from two Old English words: *crocs*, 'a clearing' and *leah*, 'a forest'. So, 'Croxley' means 'a clearing in the forest'.

CUSTOM HOUSE E16
Docklands
Opened on 28 March 1994

The area known as Custom House is named after the custom house which was situated on the north side of the Victoria Dock. It was an area developed for housing from about 1880, but was very badly damaged in the Blitz during the Second World War. The Docklands Light Railway Station is named after this area.

CUTTY SARK SE10
Docklands
Opened on 3 December 1999

The station is named after the historic merchant clipper the *Cutty Sark*, launched in 1869 and now on permanent exhibition in Greenwich. It was used in the Australian tea trade and made some very fast return journeys from Australia to the UK – seventy-three days in 1885 and sixty-nine days in 1888.

In modern English, we would refer to a *Cutty Sark* as a 'mini-skirt'! The ship got its name from the witch in Robert Burns' poem 'Tam o' Shanter' (1791), which was written in a Scottish idiom. The witch wore just a 'cutty sark' – a short shift or smock. Burns described it in the poem as 'in longitude tho' sorely scanty'. She must have been a deliciously tempting sight for sailors!

Within walking distance: Greenwich
                           The National Maritime Museum
                           The Queen's House
                           The Royal Observatory

CYPRUS E16
Docklands
Opened on 28 March 1994

Britain acquired Cyprus as a colony in 1878 (since 1960 it has been an independent republic within the British Commonwealth). Three years after this acquisition, in 1881, a housing estate known as the Cyprus Estate was built near here for workers at the Royal Albert Dock. The Docklands station Cyprus is named after the Cyprus Estate.

DAGENHAM EAST ESSEX
District
Opened as DAGENHAM by the London, Tilbury & Southend Railway on
*   1 May 1885*
First used by Underground trains on 2 June 1902
Name changed to DAGENHAM EAST on 1 May 1949

DAGENHAM HEATHWAY ESSEX
District
Opened as HEATHWAY on 12 September 1932
Name changed to DAGENHAM HEATHWAY on May 1949

'Daecca's village or homestead'. Daecca was one of the many early Saxon chieftains whose name has been perpetuated in the place where he set up his home.

DEBDEN ESSEX
Central
Opened as CHIGWELL ROAD by the Great Eastern Railway on
*   24 April 1865*
Name changed to CHIGWELL LANE on 1 December 1865
Finally changed to DEBDEN and first used by Underground trains on
*   25 September 1949*

'Debden' means 'deep valley', and derives from two Old English words: *deb*, 'deep' and *den*, 'valley'.

DEPTFORD BRIDGE SE8
Docklands
Opened on 20 November 1999

Deptford is the 'deep ford' that once existed to cross the little River Ravensbourne – a tributary of the Thames. Chaucer called it Depeford.

DEVONS ROAD E3
Docklands
Opened on 31 August 1987

Devons Road passes over this Docklands Light Railway station with a bridge at the northern end. Clearly, the station name derives from the road, and the road itself probably got its name from a Thomas Devon who once owned land in this area.

DOLLIS HILL NW2
Jubilee
Opened on 1 October 1909

In the sixteenth century this area was called Daleson Hill, probably after a local resident. Later, it became Dolly's Hill, but in 1909, when the Metropolitan Railway Station was built there, Dollis Hill became the final version.

EALING BROADWAY W5
District, Central
District Line opened on 1 July 1879
Central Line opened on 3 August 1920

EALING COMMON
District, Piccadilly
Opened on 1 July 1879

The name Ealing is Saxon and tells us that this was 'the place where Gilla's people live'.

EARLS COURT SW5
District, Piccadilly
Opened on 30 October 1871

The earls of Oxford were lords of a manor house or 'court' here until the sixteenth century. The house stood on the site between the present Barkston Gardens and Bramham Gardens. The hamlet that grew up round the 'court' naturally became known as Earl's Court.

'BUMPER HARRIS' AND HIS WOODEN LEG

The first railway escalator was installed at Earls Court Underground Station in 1911. Nervous passengers were so suspicious of this new-fangled device that the station authorities employed a man with a wooden leg – nicknamed 'Bumper' Harris – to travel up and down the escalator all day long, just to show everyone how safe it was!

EAST ACTON W3
Central   (see ACTON)
Opened on 3 August 1920

EASTCOTE MIDDLESEX
Metropolitan, Piccadilly
Opened on 26 May 1906

Former meanings of 'cot' included a cottage or a shelter for sheep
and other animals. 'Eastcote', therefore, means 'shelter in the east'.

EAST FINCHLEY N2
Northern   (see FINCHLEY)
Opened as a train station called EAST END, FINCHLEY on 22 August 1867
Name changed to EAST FINCHLEY on 1 February 1887
First used by Underground trains on 3 July 1939

EAST HAM E6
District, Hammersmith & City
Opened by London, Tilbury & Southend Railway on 31 March 1858
First used by Underground trains on 2 June 1902

East Ham was an ancient parish that existed long before it became
engulfed in the spreading housing development of London. The Old
English word *hamm* meant 'a low-lying water-meadow', so this village
gained its name from the marshy lands some distance from West Ham.

EAST INDIA E14
Docklands
Opened on 28 March 1994

This station takes its name from the East India Dock, which in turn
was named because it was used by the large ships of the East India
Company, which was founded in 1600 to trade with the Far East.
The famous clipper *Cutty Sark*, launched in 1869, used to berth in
the East India Dock, which finally closed in 1967.

EAST PUTNEY SW15
District   (see PUTNEY BRIDGE)
Opened on 3 June 1889

EDGWARE ROAD W2
Bakerloo   (see EDGWARE)
Opened on 15 June 1907

EDGWARE ROAD W2
Circle, District, Hammersmith & City   (see EDGWARE)
Opened on 1 October 1863

EDGWARE MIDDLESEX
Northern
Opened on 18 August 1924

Somewhat confusingly, there are two quite separate Underground stations both named Edgware Road and both with entrances on the Edgware Road. They are only about 150 metres apart – but they are on different Underground lines.

Then, quite separately from these, there is *another* station, simply called Edgware, at the end of the Northern Line in Middlesex. The actual Edgware Road gets its name because it leads to the town of Edgware.

As a name, Edgware has an interesting derivation, coming from the name of a Saxon farmer called Ecgi who must have built – or at least possessed – a weir. The place is named after Ecgi's weir, which was probably a fishing enclosure in the local stream.

ELEPHANT AND CASTLE SE1
Bakerloo, Northern
Northern Line opened on 18 December 1890
Bakerloo Line opened on 5 August 1906

The Underground station is named after the pub that stands near the meeting point of the roads to Kennington, Walworth and Lambeth.

Originally, the site was occupied by a smithy, but this was converted to a tavern around the year 1760, and it then became a well-known terminus for stagecoaches in the eighteenth and nineteenth centuries.

The odd name probably comes from the figure found on the sign of the Cutlers' Company, which used ivory in its manufacture of knife handles. The sign depicted a traditional medieval picture of an elephant with a castle on its back – presumably to show how huge and strong this extraordinary foreign beast was.

It has been suggested that the origin of Elephant and Castle is a badly pronounced version of 'Infanta of Castile', but this is false folk etymology.

The gaudy gilt model of an elephant with a castle on its back which once adorned the old pub, is now to be seen inside the Elephant and Castle Shopping Centre, opened in 1965.

Within walking distance: Imperial War Museum

ELM PARK ESSEX
District
Opened on 13 May 1935

The name speaks for itself. There are many streets named after trees in this neighbourhood.

ELVERSON ROAD SE8
Docklands
Opened on 20 November 1999

Elverson Road is named after one of the roads nearby, but the origin of the name is obscure, possibly deriving from a local person.

EMBANKMENT WC2
Bakerloo, Circle, District, Northern
District Line opened as CHARING CROSS on 30 May 1870
(See below for comment on subsequent name)

Sir Joseph Bazalgette, Chief Engineer of the Metropolitan Board of Works, constructed the Victoria, Albert and Chelsea embankments between 1868 and 1874, thus for the first time in London's history providing the banks of the Thames with a firm protective wall. It was an immense undertaking, with a total of 3½ miles (5.63 kilometres) of embankment, reclaiming 32 acres of swampy riverside mud.

Today we take this neat river edge for granted, and hardly give it a second thought, but until the embankments were built, London was a very different place – the Thames sprawled its muddy edges right up to the Strand.

Charles Dickens, who died in 1870, could never have seen the completed Embankments, and all his descriptions of London refer to the muddy squalor that existed before Bazalgette tidied up the riverbanks.

When Embankment Underground Station opened in May 1870 it was named Charing Cross. The Victoria Embankment itself was declared open just a few weeks later, in July of that year. Over the next century, the name of the Underground station has changed several times, and it wasn't until 12 September 1976 that it finally settled on its present name – Embankment.

EPPING E11
Central
Opened by the Great Eastern Railway on 24 April 1865
First used by Underground trains on 25 September 1949

The name is derived from the Saxon word *yppe*, meaning 'raised place' or 'look-out point', and *ing*, meaning 'people'. It is thought that the 'raised place' may refer to the Iron Age hill fort known as Ambersbury Banks in Epping Forest, where Boadicea (Boudicca) fought her last battle against the Romans.

EUSTON NW1
Northern, Victoria   (see EUSTON SQUARE)
Opened on 12 May 1907

EUSTON SQUARE NW1
Circle, Hammersmith & City, Metropolitan
Opened as GOWER STREET on 10 January 1863
Name changed to EUSTON SQUARE on 1 November 1909

The village of Euston, a few miles south of Thetford in Suffolk, indirectly gives its name to Euston Road, Euston Square and

Euston Station, the earliest of London's main-line railway termini – which opened on 20 July 1837, exactly a month after Victoria became queen.

The Fitzroy family (descended from one of Charles II's many illegitimate sons by Barbara Palmer, Duchess of Cleveland) were titled the Dukes of Grafton and Earls of Euston – in fact, the 11th Duke still lives in Euston Hall near Thetford, which is, at times, open to the public.

In the eighteenth century the Euston family owned much of this area in London. It's difficult to imagine it now, but in those days flocks of sheep and herds of cattle were constantly being driven along Oxford Street to Smithfield Market. The animals became such a nuisance that in 1756 the then Duke of Grafton had the bright idea of constructing an alternative road parallel to Oxford Street to the north, to take this farming traffic. At first this was called New Road, but it was officially renamed Euston Road in 1857, because by then Euston Station and Euston Square had been built, and Euston Road seemed a more appropriate name for a road that was no longer 'new'.

EUSTON SQUARE – THE BEGINNING OF IT ALL!

Euston Square has the distinction of being the site of the very first shaft to be sunk in the ground anywhere in the world in order to build an underground railway. This momentous event took place in January 1860, and was the first stage in constructing the Metropolitan Railway from Paddington to Farringdon.

No one could have guessed at the time just how important underground railways would become.

It is estimated that 1,000 slum homes were demolished in order to cut the first 4-mile (6.43-kilometre) stretch of the Metropolitan Line, linking Paddington, Euston Square, St Pancras, King's Cross and Farringdon. About 12,000 people had to be displaced.

The original Euston Square Station, which opened for overground trains in 1837.

FAIRLOP ESSEX
Central
Opened by the Great Eastern Railway on 1 May 1903
First used by Underground trains on 31 May 1948

A gigantic tree once grew here known as the Fairlop Oak and a popular annual fair used to take place around it every July. The word 'lop' refers to a lopped tree. This famous oak tree, associated with the fair, measured 48½ feet (14.78 metres) round its trunk and was reputed to be almost 1,000 years old. Sadly, it was cut down in 1820, but a part of it still remains, as the pulpit in St Pancras' church, which is carved from a portion of its boughs.

Other Underground 'tree names' include Becontree and Burnt Oak. The trees may have gone, but their names live on.

FARRINGDON EC1
Circle, Hammersmith & City, Metropolitan
Opened as FARRINGDON STREET on 10 January 1863
Name changed to FARRINGDON & HIGH HOLBORN on 26 January 1922
Finally became simply FARRINGTON on 21 April 1936

When this station opened on 10 January 1863 (an important date – see below) it was named Farringdon Street, a road that was built in 1845–46 and still exists. The road was named after

Farringdon Ward, which in turn was named after two aldermen of the City of London, William and Nicholas de Farndon, who lived in the thirteenth century.

FARRINGDON STREET TO PADDINGTON – THE WORLD'S FIRST UNDERGROUND JOURNEY

At 6 am on 10 January 1863, the world's very first underground train took passengers along its 4-mile journey (6.43-kilometre) from Farringdon Street Station to Paddington. There were seven stations, including the two termini, in this first stretch of the Metropolitan Line.

The steam-driven locomotive pulled its passengers along in first-, second- and third-class carriages – lit with gas so that 'newspapers might be read with ease'.

Naming a new invention is always an interesting task, and the chosen word, 'Metropolitan' comes from two ancient Greek words meaning 'mother city', referring, of course, to London.

The venture was so successful, and the 'Metropolitan' gained such fame and prestige that it became the standard name for underground railways in other countries as they took up the idea.

Both the Paris Metro and the Russian Metro take their name from this pioneering first Underground line in London.

FINCHLEY CENTRAL N3
Central   (see FINCHLEY ROAD)

Opened by the Great Northern Railway as FINCHEY & HENDON on 22 August 1867

Name changed to FINCHLEY (CHURCH END) on 1 February 1894

Finally changed to FINCHLEY CENTRAL on 1 April 1940

First used by Underground trains on 14 April 1940

Entrance to Clerkenwell tunnel from Farringdon Street.

FINCHLEY ROAD NW2
Jubilee, Metropolitan
Opened on 30 June 1879

'Finchley' is a reminder of those days when this was a completely
rural area. Its Saxon name means 'wood where finches are to
be found'.

FINSBURY PARK N4
Piccadilly, Victoria
Opened by the Great Northern Railway as SEVEN SISTERS ROAD on 1 July 1861
Name changed to FINSBURY PARK in 1869
First used by Underground trains on 15 December 1906

'Finsbury' means 'settlement belonging to Finn' – one of the innumerable Saxon chiefs who have left their memorial within the name of the place where they settled.

Finsbury Park used to be called Stroud Green, *stroud* being an Old English word meaning 'marshy land overgrown with brushwood'.

It was not until 1869 that Finsbury Park came into existence. It was named after the district of Finsbury, whose inhabitants wanted an open space or park. It was specially purchased for recreational use, and Finsbury Park became one of the first municipal parks in the country.

FULHAM BROADWAY SW6
District
Opened as WALHAM GREEN on 1 March 1880
Name changed to FULHAM BROADWAY on 2 March 1952

The place where a Saxon chief called Fulla settled with his family and friends. The 'hamm' part of the name means low-lying land in the bend of a river.

GALLIONS REACH E16
Docklands
Opened on 28 March 1994

Gallions Reach Station is named after a stretch of the Thames between Woolwich and Barking Creek – Gallions Point, at the entrance to the King George V Dock. The name is derived from the Galyons, a fourteenth-century family who owned property on this shoreline.

GANTS HILL ESSEX
Central
Opened on 14 December 1947

Named after Richard le Gant, or perhaps one of his relations.
He lived here in the late thirteenth century. The area was called
Gantesgrave in 1291 and Gauntes Hethe in 1545.

GLOUCESTER ROAD SW7
Circle, District, Piccadilly
Opened as BROMPTON (GLOUCESTER ROAD) on 1 October 1868
Name changed to GLOUCESTER ROAD in 1907

Gloucester Road itself was built in 1826, and was named after Maria,
Duchess of Gloucester, who secretly married a brother of King
George III. She had bought a house, Orford Lodge, on the site of
what is now Stanhope Gardens. The road was named soon after the
Duchess died. Formerly, it had been just a track called Hogmore
Lane.

The very first trial trip on the London underground in 1863.

GOLDERS GREEN NW11
Northern
Opened on 22 June 1907

The name comes from a local landowner, and was first recorded as Golders Greene in 1612. At that time it was just a green field in Middlesex, and it remained totally undeveloped until the coming of the underground railway in the early twentieth century.

GOLDHAWK ROAD W6
Hammersmith & City
Opened on 1 April 1914

Named after fourteenth-century farmer John Goldhawk of Sands End, whose family continued to hold several plots of land in this area for many generations.

GOODGE STREET W1
Northern
Opened as TOTTENHAM COURT ROAD on 22 June 1907
Name changed to GOODGE STREET on 9 March 1908

In the eighteenth century this land was called Crab Tree Field and Walnut Tree Field. It belonged to a carpenter called John Goodge. On his death in 1748, his nephews Francis and William Goodge developed the land for building.

GRANGE HILL ESSEX
Central
Opened by the Great Eastern Railway on 1 May 1903
First used by Underground trains on 21 November 1948

In the Middle Ages a 'grange' meant an outlying farm, often belonging to a monastery or nearby religious community. In this case, the 'grange' belonged to Tilty Priory, but after Henry VIII's dissolution of the monasteries it ultimately became a part of Brentwood Grammar School. It was finally demolished in the late nineteenth century. The 'hill' leads down to the front of the station.

GREAT PORTLAND STREET W1
Circle, Hammersmith & City, Metropolitan
Opened as PORTLAND ROAD on 10 January 1863
Name changed to PORTLAND STREET on 1 March 1917

Great Portland Street was built in the eighteenth century, and given its name because it was on land owned by the second Duke of Portland.

GREENFORD MIDDLESEX
Central
Opened by the Great Western Railway on 1 October 1904
First used, in a new station, by Underground trains on 30 June 1947

A place by a 'green ford' – a useful crossing-place through the river Brent. The name goes back to Saxon times and was recorded as Greneforde in 1066.

GREEN PARK SW1
Jubilee, Piccadilly, Victoria
Opened as DOVER STREET on 15 December 1906
Name changed to GREEN PARK on 18 September 1933

Green Park itself, after which the Underground station is called, consists of 53 acres of green lawns and green trees, so it is appropriately named. It is believed to have been the burial place of the lepers who used to live in the former Hospital of St James's, the site of which was used by Henry VIII to build St James's Palace.

The name *Green* Park was given because no flowers are planted there, the reason for this being that it was a burial area. In the eighteenth century it was a favourite place for duelling, and it was also a haunt of highwaymen.

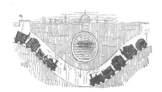

Within walking distance: Buckingham Palace
                            Royal Mews
                            Queen's Gallery
                            Royal Academy of Arts
                            St James's Piccadilly
                            St James's Palace
                            Spencer House

GREENWICH SW10
Docklands
Opened on 11 November 1994

Greenwich, with its palace and its observatory, has played an immensely important role in English history and has witnessed many extraordinary events from Saxon times onwards. The name means 'green port' or 'landing place'. The Old English word *wic* in this name means 'harbour'.

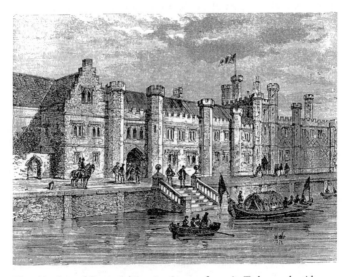

The old palace of Greenwich in 1630. It was a favourite Tudor royal residence, and Elizabeth I was born there.

GUNNERSBURY MIDDLESEX
District
Opened by the London & South Western Railway as BRENTFORD ROAD
*   on 1 January 1869*
Name changed to GUNNERSBURY on 1 November 1871
First used by Underground trains on 1 June 1877

Gunnersbury House and Gunnersbury Park, which give this station
its name, are possibly derived from Gunhilda, a niece of King
Canute (reigned 1016–35) who lived in a manor house here until
she was banished from England in 1044. 'Gunnersbury' means 'the
manor of Gunhilda'.

HAINAULT FOREST ESSEX
Central
Opened by the Great Eastern Railway on 1 May 1903
First used by Underground trains on 31 May 1948

The name of this part of the Royal Forest of Essex means 'wood
belonging to a monastic community' – from the Old English *higna*,
'household', and *holt*, 'wood' – and the community referred to was
that of Barking Abbey.

Despite the apparent link with Edward III's queen – Philippa of
Hainault – there is no connection at all with this Flemish name.

HAMMERSMITH W6
District, Hammersmith & City, Piccadilly
Hammersmith & City Line opened on 13 June 1864
District and Piccadilly lines opened on 9 September 1874

The first record of this name – as Hammersmyth – was in 1294.
There must have been a smithy here with a good, resounding
hammer. The words are so fundamental to that basic tool and trade
that they have remained unchanged for well over 700 years.

HAMPSTEAD NW3
Northern
Opened on 22 June 1907

Hampstead is simply a Saxon word meaning 'homestead'. Its first recorded use was in AD 959, as Hemstede. It is the deepest Underground station in London – at 192 feet (58.5 metres) below ground level.

HANGER LANE W5
Central
Opened on 30 June 1947

Hanger was a Saxon word for a slope – often a wooded slope. It is quite a common part of English place names such as Clayhanger in Cheshire, Oakhanger in Hampshire and Hartanger (stag slope) in Kent.

HARLESDEN NW10
Bakerloo
Opened by the London & North Western Railway on 15 June 1912
First used by Underground trains on 16 April 1917

This name ultimately comes from the Old English *Herewulf's tun*. Herewulf must have been a Saxon chief, and his *tun* was a farm or settlement.

HARROW & WEALDSTONE MIDDLESEX
Bakerloo
Opened by the London & Birmingham Railway as HARROW on 20 July 1837
Name changed to HARROW & WEALDSTONE on 1 May 1897
First used by Underground trains on 16 April 1917

The 'Harrow' in this name comes from a Saxon word *hearg*, meaning 'shrine' or 'temple'. The earliest record of this name dates back to

AD 767, when it was known as *Gumeninga hergae*, or 'temples of the Gumeningas', the name of an early tribe of settlers.

There is no relic from this original shrine but the lovely Church of St Mary in Harrow-on-the-Hill may well stand on the site, as Christian missionaries were urged to turn heathen temples into churches by Pope Gregory the Great.

Wealdstone refers to the Harrow Weald boundary stone – a boundary mark separating Harrow Weald from the parish of Harrow itself. 'Weald' means 'forest' or 'woodland'.

HARROW-ON-THE-HILL MIDDLESEX
Metropolitan   (see HARROW & WEALDSTON)
Opened as HARROW on 2 August 1880
Name changed to HARROW-ON-THE-HILL on 1 June 1894

HATTON CROSS MIDDLESEX
Piccadilly
Opened on 19 July 1975

There are many places called Hatton in Britain. It is a Saxon name meaning a *tun*, or 'settlement on the heath'. The 'cross' refers to a road junction there.

HEATHROW MIDDLESEX
Piccadilly
Terminals 1, 2, 3 opened as HEATHROW CENTRAL on 16 December 1976
Name changed to HEATHROW CENTRAL TERMINALS 1, 2, 3 on
*   3 October 1983*
Changed again to HEATHROW (Terminals 1, 2, 3) on 12 April 1986
HEATHROW TERMINAL 4 opened on 12 April 1986
HEATHROW TERMINAL 5 opened on 27 March 2008

Today this name is inseparable from the airport, one of the busiest in the world. Originally, it simply meant a row of dwellings near a heath – in this case, Hounslow Heath. Gatwick, the airport further away from London, has an equally rural meaning –'goat farm'.

HENDON CENTRAL NW4
Northern
Opened on 19 November 1923

'High hill' stems from the Saxon words *haeh dune*, a 'high dun' or 'hill'.

HERON QUAYS E14
Docklands
Opened on 31 August 1987

The name refers to herons – long-necked wading birds – which used to nest on the buildings here, and which can sometimes still be seen in this dockland area.

HIGH BARNET HERTFORDSHIRE
Northern
Opened by the Great Northern Railway on 1 April 1872
First used by Underground trains on 14 April 1940

The Saxon word *baernet* meant a 'burning' – in other words, a clearing in the forest made by burning the trees and undergrowth.

THE BLOODY BATTLE OF BARNET

It was on Easter Sunday, 14 April 1471, that the bloody Battle of Barnet took place between the opposing forces of the Yorkists and the Lancastrians in one of the final clashes in the Wars of the Roses. At that time there were two rival kings of England – Henry VI and Edward IV.

Henry VI – a Lancastrian – had been taken prisoner by Edward IV, and was taken captive to Barnet to watch his supporters, led by the Earl of Warwick, being butchered by Edward's Yorkist troops. Much of the fighting took place in dense fog, adding greatly to the confusion.

The Earl of Warwick and his brother were both slain, and their bodies were taken back to London to be publicly displayed outside Old St Paul's Cathedral. Henry VI was taken back to the Tower of London to be murdered. And Edward IV went on to win another battle shortly afterwards at Tewkesbury, killing Henry VI's son, the then Prince of Wales, after which he settled himself firmly on the throne without any fear of further opposition.

The three-hour battle was fought on Hadley Green, a little to the north of High Barnet.

HIGHBURY & ISLINGTON N6
Victoria
Opened as HIGHBURY on 28 June 1904
Named changed to HIGHBURY & ISLINGTON on 20 July 1922

'Highbury' means 'high manor' – so called because it was built on higher ground than its two neighbouring manors, Canonbury and Barnsbury.

'Islington' means 'Gisla's hill' – Gisla is the personal name of some Saxon chief, with the addition of dune ('hill') as a suffix.

HIGHGATE N6
Northern
Opened by the Great Northern Railway on 22 August 1867
First used by Underground trains on 19 January 1941

This area once belonged to the bishops of London. In the fourteenth century one of the bishops allowed a road to be built over the hill, but he made a profit for himself by erecting toll gates along it. Highgate gets its name from the toll gate which stood at the top of the hill.

Tradition has it that Dick Whittington rested at the bottom of Highgate Hill and heard Bow Bells ring out the famous message:

Turn again, Whittington,
Thrice Lord Mayor of London Town.

HIGH STREET KENSINGTON W8
Circle, District   (see KENSINGTON (OLYMPIA))

Opened on 1 October 1868

Within walking distance: Kensington Gardens
                            Kensington Palace

HILLINGDON MIDDLESEX
Piccadilly, Metropolitan

Opened on 10 December 1923

This is a Saxon name meaning the *dun*, or 'hill', where a man with a name something like Hilla, Hildric or Hildwulf lived.

HOLBORN EC1
Central, Piccadilly

Piccadilly Line opened on 15 December 1906
Central Line platforms opened on 25 September 1933

The upper part of the Fleet river used to be called the *Hole-bourne*, or 'stream in the hollow'.

A rustic view of Highgate as it was in 1745.

Nowadays, somewhat ignominiously, this stream is diverted into the Thames in an underground pipe, and few people are aware of the rivulet that gives this part of London its name.

Within walking distance: The British Museum
                               The Courtauld Gallery
                               (Somerset House)
                               Inns of Court
                               Sir John Soane's Museum
                               The Old Curiosity Shop

HOLLAND PARK W11
Central
Opened on 30 July 1900

This Underground station is named after Holland House, a large and beautiful Jacobean house in Kensington, with adjoining grounds called Holland Park. It was owned by Henry Rich, who became Earl of Holland in 1624.

The widow of the third Earl of Holland married the writer Joseph Addison, who wrote many of his essays for the *Spectator* in Holland House. In the long gallery there, Addison composed his writings by walking up and down and placing a bottle of wine at each end, so that he could refresh his mind at regular intervals.

Sadly, the house was largely destroyed by bombing during the Second World War.

HOLLOWAY ROAD N17
Piccadilly
Opened on 15 December 1906

In former times the name holloway referred to the fact that the road was low-lying and boggy – the 'hollow way'.

"... A TERROR TO EVIL DOERS"

The famous Holloway Prison was opened in 1852 for both men and women, and originally known as The City House of Correction. Since 1902 it has been used exclusively for women. Mrs Emmeline Pankhurst, leader of the Suffragettes' campaigning for women's rights, was imprisoned here, together with fellow female campaigners.

Although the buildings have been redesigned, the original glass foundation stone remains, with its formidable inscription: 'May God preserve the City of London and make this place a terror to evil doers'.

HORNCHURCH ESSEX
District
Opened by the London, Tilbury & Southend Railway on 1 May 1885
First used by Underground trains on 2 June 1902

The origin of this name is obscure. A fourteenth-century manuscript gives the name as Hornedecherche, so it has been suggested that this 'horned church' meant 'church with the horn-like gables'.

This odd carving of a bull's head is on the exterior of St Andrew's, Hornchurch, and gives the town its name.

On the eastern gable end of St Andrew's church in Hornchurch is a wooden carving of a bull's head with a pair of magnificent copper-plated horns. It was placed there in the eighteenth century but there must have been an earlier tradition of horns attached to this 'horned church'. Could it be an association with some pre-Christian cult? It is an odd mystery.

HOUNSLOW CENTRAL MIDDLESEX
Piccadilly
Opened as HESTON HOUNSLOW on 1 April 1886
Name changed to HOUNSLOW CENTRAL on 1 December 1925

HOUNSLOW EAST MIDDLESEX
Piccadilly   (see HOUNSLOW CENTRAL)
Opened as HOUNSLOW on 1 May 1883
Name changed to HOUNSLOW TOWN in 1884 (closed 1886)
New station opened on 2 May 1909
Finally named HOUNSLOW EAST on 1 December 1925

HOUNSLOW WEST MIDDLESEX
Piccadilly   (see HOUNSLOW CENTRAL)
Opened as HOUNSLOW BARRACKS on 21 July 1884
Name changed to HOUNSLOW WEST on 1 December 1925
New station opened on 11 December 1926

In Old English, a *lawe* was a piece of rising land or a barrow, so the earlier form of Hounslow was Hundeslawe, a hill where a man named Hund may have lived – though it has been suggested (incorrectly) that it was a place where dogs (hounds) were to be found.

The first mention of the name of the town of Hounslow appears in the year of Magna Carta, 1215, when, after the signing of the charter, the barons held a celebration in the form of a tournament in Staines Wood, and at Hounslow itself.

HYDE PARK CORNER SW1
Piccadilly
Opened on 15 December 1906

Shortly after the Norman Conquest in 1066, Geoffrey de Mandeville bequeathed three extensive properties, Ebury, Neate and Hyde, to the monks of Westminster.

Almost six centuries later, when Henry VIII destroyed all the monasteries, he sold the first two, but kept the manor and lands of Hyde for himself as a hunting ground.

It's difficult to imagine that deer, wild boar and wild bulls were to be found here, but deer were still being hunted here in the park as late as 1768.

The name Hyde is interesting, as it was an area of land that could support a single family – i.e. between 60 and 120 acres (24–49 hectares) depending on the quality of the land – and it is linked with the Old English word *hiw*, 'family' or 'household'. It is likely that the original property consisted of just one 'hyde'.

Within walking distance: Apsley House (Wellington Museum)
                               Buckingham Palace
                               Constitution Arch
                               Hyde Park
                               The Queen's Gallery
                               Royal Mews
                               Wellington Monument

ICKENHAM MIDDLESEX
Metropolitan, Piccadilly
Opened as ICKENHAM HALT on 25 September 1905

'Ticca's village'. This name has lost its first letter 't', probably because of the phrase 'at Ticca's ham' (village). Said quickly, the two 't's merge together and over time it became simply 'at Icca's ham' – hence, 'Ickenham'. Ticca was another of those innumerable Saxon chieftains whose existence is inferred only by a place name.

ISLAND GARDENS E14
Docklands
Opened on 31 August 1987

The island referred to is the Isle of Dogs. This is not a proper
island, but is the peninsula within the big bend in the river Thames
opposite Greenwich. The origin of the name has never been finally
explained – but it may be that it is derived from the fact that
Edward III (reigned 1327–77) kept his royal kennels here. Another
explanation is that it is a corruption of Isle of Ducks – a reference to
the wildfowl that once inhabited the marshes here. Alternatively, it
may have been just a rude term of contempt.

   More directly, Island Gardens is a reference to a park named Island
Garden, opened here in 1895 by the London County Council.

KENNINGTON SE11
Northern
Opened on 18 December 1890

'Kennington' probably derives from the name of a Saxon chief
known as Cœna and means 'the farm or estate of Cœna's people'.

A placid scene in rural Kennington, in 1780.

Alternatively, there is a possibility that it may derive from the Old English *kynig-tun*, or 'king's town', for it was once a royal manor. The Black Prince (1330–78), son of Edward III – given his strange nickname because of his black armour – had a palace in this area, which was used as a royal residence until the reign of Henry VII. This association with the Black Prince is kept alive in the name of Black Prince Road, running from the Embankment to Kennington Road.

Charles I (reigned 1625–49) lived for a while in a house built on the site of the Black Prince's palace. No trace of these old buildings now remain, but a part of the former grounds of the palace is now taken up by the Oval Cricket Ground, which is within walking distance of this station.

KENSAL GREEN NW10
Northern
Opened on 1 October 1916

'Kensal' is derived from the Old English word *Kingisholt*, meaning 'King's wood' – so 'Kensal Green' means 'clearing in the King's forest'.

KENSINGTON (OLYMPIA) W6
District
Opened by the West London Railway as KENSINGTON on 27 May 1844
Site moved on 2 June 1862
Name changed to KENSINGTON (ADDISON ROAD) in 1868
Name finally changed to KENSINGTON (OLYMPIA) on 19 December 1946

Kensington is derived from Cynesige's *tun*, or 'farm'. In 1086 the Domesday Book referred to it as Cheninton. For Olympia, see below.

'OLYMPIA' – 10 YEARS BEFORE THE FIRST OLYMPIC GAMES!

London had its 'Olympia' here ten years before the first modern Olympic Games took place in 1896.

Olympia on the Hammersmith Road was built on the site of a large former nursery garden, and was originally called The National Agricultural Hall.

When the Paris Hippodrome circus came to perform here in 1886, with 400 animals, a chariot race and a stag hunt, it was felt that the venue needed a more exciting name – so Olympia was proposed and adopted – with reference to the famous Greek games of antiquity.

It has been the scene of circuses, shows and exhibitions ever since.

KENTISH TOWN NW5
Northern
Opened on 22 June 1907

The obvious meaning might seem to be that this is a town where Kentish people settled – but this would be wrong. Here, the name is probably derived from a farm or estate belonging to someone called Le Kentish. It was recorded as Kentisston in 1208.

Coach and horses approaching an old pub in Kentish Town in 1820.

KENTON MIDDLESEX
Bakerloo
Opened by the London & North Western Railway on 15 June 1912
First used by Underground trains on 16 April 1917

There is a similarity between Kenton and Kennington in that both places are derived from the name of a Saxon leader named Coena, and *tun* refers to the farm or homestead where he lived. Whether they were one and the same person is impossible to tell after this length of time.

KEW GARDENS SURREY
District
Opened by the London & South Western Railway on 1 January 1869
First used by Underground trains on 1 June 1877

Kew gets its name from its situation on the Thames. It means 'quay' or 'wharf'.

The 'Gardens' part of the name refers to the Royal Botanic Gardens, now a world famous scientific centre and popular pleasure garden, which attracts many thousands of visitors annually.

The gardens were the grounds of a small palace – or 'wonderful country house' as Prince Charles calls it – renovated and re-opened to the public in 2006. It was a favourite residence of King George III (reigned 1760–1820) and Queen Adelaide. The house and gardens were given to the nation by Queen Victoria in 1841, as she had taken up residence in her new home in Buckingham Palace.

Within walking distance: Royal Botanic Gardens

KILBURN NW6
Jubilee
Opened as KILBURN & BRONDESBURY on 24 November 1879
Name changed to KILBURN on 25 September 1950

Kilburn may be derived from the Saxon *cylenburne*, meaning 'stream by a kiln', or alternatively 'place near a stream where cattle graze'.

KILBURN PARK NW6
Bakerloo   (see KILBURN)
Opened on 31 January 1915

KING GEORGE V SE9
Docklands
Opened on 2 December 2005

This station is named after King George V Dock, the third of the royal docks. King George V himself (reigned 1910–35) officially opened this dock in 1921. It was built to enhance and extend the trade that was passing through the two other royal docks – the Royal Victoria and the Royal Albert. The King George V Dock was closed in 1981.

KINGSBURY NW9
Jubilee
Opened on 10 December 1932

'The king's burg'. This is an old name, dating from Saxon times, before the Norman Conquest. It was recorded as *Kynges byrig* in 1046. A *burg* was a fortified place, stronghold or manor. The Saxon king, Edward the Confessor (reigned 1042–66) gave this Kingsbury to the monks of Westminster Abbey in 1044.

The antiquity of this name contrasts greatly with that of Queensbury, the next station along the Jubilee Line to Stanmore. (See QUEENSBURY)

KING'S CROSS ST PANCRAS NW1
Circle, Hammersmith & City, Metropolitan, Northern, Piccadilly, Victoria
Metropolitan Line opened as KING'S CROSS on 10 January 1863
Piccadilly Line opened on 15 December 1906
Northern Line opened on 12 May 1907
Name changed to KING'S CROSS & ST PANCRAS in 1925
Name changed imperceptibly to KING'S CROSS for ST PANCRAS in 1927
Name changed sensibly to KING'S CROSS ST PANCRAS in 1933

After much reconstruction to include the Victoria Line, the present station
  opened on 1 December 1968

King's Cross is a comparatively recent name, compared with, say, Charing Cross. The king referred to is George IV (reigned 1820–30). Six years after his death, a 60-feet (18.29-metre) high monument was erected at the junction of Euston, Pentonville, St Pancras and Gray's Inn roads. On top of this was a statue of George IV. This odd-looking monument was used first as a police station and then as a public house.

The whole monstrosity was so unpopular that the king's statue was removed after only six years and the monument itself was demolished in 1845.

However, the name King's Cross hung around in people's memories, and became used for the railway station, which was built a few years later, in 1851–52. (See ST PANCRAS)

The strange monument which carried a statue of George IV on top – thus giving the name 'King's Cross' to the area.

KNIGHTSBRIDGE SW1
Piccadilly
Opened on 15 December 1906

The name is so famous and so frequently used that few people ever question what it means or take it literally as the 'knights' bridge'.

Legend has it that two knights fought here on a bridge that spanned the river Westbourne. According to this old story, the two knights both fell into the river and were drowned. Since then, so it is said, the bridge and the former village nearby took the name of Knightsbridge. How true this is, no one will ever know – but it is an intriguing old tale. The name was recorded as Cnihtebricge during the reign of King Edward the Confessor (reigned 1042–66).

The river Westbourne was 'tamed' in the eighteenth century to form the Serpentine in Hyde Park. From there it is now taken, somewhat ignominiously, down to the Thames in a large conduit. En route, the conduit can be seen crossing the lines and above the trains at Sloane Square Underground Station.

Within walking distance: Harrods
                                        Hyde Park

LADBROKE GROVE W10
Hammersmith & City
Opened as NOTTING HILL on 13 June 1864
Name changed to NOTTING HILL & LADBROKE GROVE in 1880
Name changed again to LADBROKE GROVE (NORTH KENSINGTON) on 1 June 1919
Finally simplified to LADBROKE GROVE in 1938

All the Ladbroke names in this area refer to Richard Ladbroke, who owned two farms north of Notting Hill in the seventeenth century. The streets were laid out in the nineteenth century, when the area was sold by later generations of Ladbrokes for housing development.

LAMBETH NORTH SE1
Bakerloo
Opened as KENNINGTON ROAD on 10 March 1906
Name changed to WESTMINSTER BRIDGE ROAD on 5 August 1906
Finally changed to LAMBETH NORTH on 15 April 1917

There are many hythes, or wharves, along the banks of the Thames, which are named after the goods that were once predominantly shipped there. Lambeth gets its name from being a 'lamb hythe' – the wharf where lambs were shipped.

Within walking distance: Imperial War Museum

LANCASTER GATE W2
Central
Opened on 30 July 1900

Named in honour of the Duchy of Lancaster. One of Queen Victoria's titles was Duchess of Lancaster, and she had been born in Kensington Palace in 1919. The beautiful Lancaster Gate itself was designed in 1857 by the architect Sancton Wood, and is situated on the north side of Kensington Gardens. All the places of interest in these gardens are easily accessible from Lancaster Gate.

Within walking distance: Hyde Park
Diana, Princess of Wales
  Memorial Fountain
Kensington Gardens
Kensington Palace
Serpentine Gallery

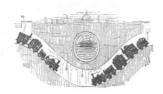

LANGDON PARK E14
Docklands
Opened on 9 December 2007

Opened in December 2007, Langdon Park is one of the very latest stations on the Docklands Light Railway. It can be found only on the most up-to-date maps of the London Underground system. It is situated between All Saints and Devons Road.

When in the planning stage, this station was provisionally called Carmen Street but then it was changed to Langdon Park, named after a local park and an adjacent secondary school, which were themselves named after the Revd C.G. Langdon, vicar of All Angels, Bromley-by-Bow between 1913 and 1925.

LATIMER ROAD BUCKINGHAMSHIRE
Hammersmith & City
Opened on 16 December 1868

In the Middle Ages this village was called Isenhampstede. But when William Latymer acquired the manor in 1330 the name changed: first to Isenhampstede Latymer and then simply to Latimer. As a surname, it signified 'someone who can speak or understand Latin'.

Leicester Square in about 1750.

LEICESTER SQUARE WC2
Northern, Piccadilly
Opened on 15 December 1906

Robert Sidney, a nephew of the famous Elizabethan poet Sir Philip Sidney, acquired the land here in the 1630s. He was the 2nd Earl of Leicester, so the house he built for himself between 1631 and 1635 on this spot naturally became known as Leicester House. Leicester Square was laid out in 1670, in front of the earl's house.

Leicester House was demolished in 1790, and its nineteenth-century replacement burnt down in 1865.

Within walking distance: National Gallery
National Portrait Gallery
St Martin-in-the-Fields
Trafalgar Square

LEWISHAM SE13
Docklands
Opened on 11 November 1999

'Leofsa's village'. In other words, the *ham*, or 'homestead', of a Saxon chief with this name.

LEYTON E10
Central
Opened as LOW LEYTON by the Eastern Counties Railway on 22 August 1856
Name changed to LEYTON on 1 January 1868
First used by Underground trains on 5 May 1947

'Farm on the river Lea' – a Saxon name.

LEYTONSTONE E11
Central
Opened as LEYTONSTONE by the Eastern Counties Railway on 22 August 1856
First used by Underground trains on 5 May 1947

This station is east of Leyton (see above) and the name means 'Leyton by the stone'. Local tradition has it that the 'stone' in this name was in fact a Roman milestone, but in any case it signifies a boundary stone of some sort.

LIMEHOUSE E14
Docklands
Opened on 31 August 1987

The lime kilns, or 'oasts', around this dockland area gave Limehouse its name – for the 'house' part is a corruption of the Old English word *ast*, meaning 'kiln'. Supplies of chalk were brought up from Kent from at least the fourteenth century onwards.

LIVERPOOL STREET EC2
Central, Circle, Hammersmith & City, Metropolitan
Opened by the Metropolitan Line as BISHOPSGATE on 12 July 1875
Name changed to LIVERPOOL STREET on 1 November 1909
Central Line opened on 28 July 1912

A twisting old street named Old Bethlem was built over in 1829 to form Liverpool Street, named in honour of Lord Liverpool, Prime Minister 1812–27. Liverpool Street Station, opened in 1874, was named after this newly built and renamed street.

SHEER BEDLAM!

The former name of Liverpool Street – Old Bethlem – referred to the Bethlem Hospital, which used to stand on the site of the present day Liverpool Street Station.

Our word 'bedlam' derives from the name of this hospital, because many of its patients were mentally deranged. It became a crude but fashionable sport among the gentry in the eighteenth century to go and watch the pathetic antics of these unfortunate inmates – all crowded together in an appalling rabble. This, indeed, was 'bedlam'.

In the final image of *The Rake's Progress*, the artist William Hogarth (1697–1764) depicts Tom Rakewell ending his wretched life in 'Bethlehem Hospital madhouse'.

LONDON BRIDGE SE1
Northern, Jubilee
Opened on 25 February 1900

The first London Bridge was built by the Romans during their occupation of Britain between AD 100 and AD 400. The Roman name for the settlement here was recorded as Londinium in *c.* AD 115 – but the origin is 'tantalizingly obscure' and is probably pre-Celtic.

Many bridges have been built over the Thames since then, but the one on this site is *the* London Bridge. Its importance can best be understood when it is remembered that until Westminster Bridge was opened in 1750, London Bridge was the *only* bridge across the Thames in London. In fact, apart from a wooden structure constructed at Putney in 1727–29, the next bridge upstream from London Bridge was the one at Kingston upon Thames, a distance of about 12 miles (20 kilometres).

One reason for the lack of bridges was the sturdy hostility of the huge number of Thames watermen, who carried passengers across and up and down the river. It is estimated that in the seventeenth century about 40,000 watermen earned their living on the river. Obviously, any bridge building was a threat to their livelihood.

The present bridge was built in 1967–72, and its immediate predecessor, built by Sir John Rennie and opened in 1831 by King William IV and Queen Adelaide, was shipped across the Atlantic in pieces and re-erected at Lake Havasu City, Arizona.

Old London Bridge as it was in 1756 – an illustration made just before the demolition of the houses built on it.

Before Rennie's bridge, many other picturesque versions of London Bridge existed, with houses and chapels along the entire length, making it impossible for traffic to pass with any ease.

Within walking distance: Clink Prison Museum
Design Museum
HMS *Belfast*
The London Dungeon
Southwark Cathedral
Tower Bridge

LOUGHTON ESSEX
Central
Opened originally by the Eastern Counties Railway on 22 August 1856
A new station opened on 28 April 1940
First used by Underground trains on 21 November 1948

The name of Loughton derives from the fact that it was the *tun*, or 'dwelling place', of Luca, a Saxon landowner.

MAIDA VALE W9
Bakerloo
Opened on 6 June 1915

The name of this district north of Paddington commemorates the almost forgotten Battle of Maida, fought in 1806 on the southern tip of Italy, in which the British, led by General Sir John Stuart, defeated the French.

'Maida' (deriving from the Italian town of San Pietro di Maida, near where this battle was fought) first came to the area soon after the victory was won, in the name of a pub on the Edgware Road called Hero of Maida. Gradually, the name of the pub was transferred to the road itself: first as Maida Hill, and then as Maida Vale.

MANOR HOUSE N4
Piccadilly
Opened on 19 September 1932

Manor House is the name of a nearby pub – and this gives the station its name.

MANSION HOUSE EC2
Circle, District
Opened on 3 July 1871

The Mansion House was specially built to be the official residence of the Lord Mayor of London, where he must reside during his year of office.

In 1735 many famous architects were asked to produce plans, but it was George Dance, Clerk of the City Works at that time, whose design was chosen. The Mansion House itself was completed in 1752.

Within walking distance: Guildhall
                              Shakespeare's Globe Theatre

MARBLE ARCH W1
Central
Opened on 30 July 1900

Marble Arch, constructed out of Carrara marble and one of the most famous landmarks in London, is rather oddly sited. John Nash, the architect who designed it, based it on the Arch of Constantine in Rome. Originally, in 1827, it was set up in front of Buckingham Palace, during the reign of George IV (reigned 1810–30). However, it did not find favour with Queen Victoria (reigned 1837–1901) and so it was moved to its present site in 1851.

George IV's intention was to have an equestrian statue of himself on top of Marble Arch, but this was never done, and the statue that was to have been used can now be seen in the north-east corner of Trafalgar Square.

Officially, only senior members of the Royal Family and the King's Troop Royal Horse Artillery are allowed to pass through it.

Within walking distance: Diana, Princess of Wales
                            Memorial Fountain
                          Hyde Park
                          Oxford Street shopping
                          Serpentine Gallery

TYBURN GALLOWS

Marble Arch stands very near the site of the most notorious place of public execution in London – Tyburn gallows. It has been estimated that about 50,000 criminals were hanged there between the twelfth century and 1783, the year when the gallows were moved to Newgate Prison. This averages a rate of about seven a month. Important 'hanging days' were public holidays as the authorities considered that the sight of people being hanged would act as a deterrent to crime.

Tyburn gallows were triangular in shape with three upright posts supporting three strong horizontal wooden beams from which the malefactors were hanged. The method of hanging was crude and brutal. A seventeenth-century visitor to London described how the hangman brought his victim under the gallows on a horse-drawn cart, then with the criminal still on the cart, tied an end of his rope around one of the crossbeams 'while the other went round the wretch's neck. This done, he gives the horse a lash with his whip, away goes the cart and there swings my gentleman, kicking in the air'.

MARYLEBONE W1
Bakerloo
Opened as GREAT CENTRAL on 27 March 1907
Name changed to MARYLEBONE on 15 April 1917

In the Middle Ages this district was known as Tyburn, named after the river Tyburn, meaning 'boundary stream'. The little Church of St Mary stood by this river and gave the village its name; various forms of it were St Mary-at-Bourne, Marybourne, Mary-by-the-Bourne, Mary-le-bone and finally the present form: Marylebone. Literally, then, it means 'St Mary's church by the boundary river'.

The rural area around present-day Marble Arch, which was the setting of Tyburn Gallows, where hundreds of criminals were hanged.

Lord Ferrers being hanged at Tyburn. He was the last member of the House of Lords to be hanged there. As he was a lord, a silken noose was used for his noble neck.

MILE END E1
Central, District, Hammersmith & City
Opened on 2 June 1902

'Mile End' means exactly what it says – it is 1 mile from the City of London – or, more accurately, from Aldgate. A medieval hamlet existed here just about where Mile End meets Globe Road.

MILL HILL EAST NW7
Northern
Opened as MILL HILL by the Great Northern Railway on 22 August 1867
Name changed to MILL HILL EAST on 1 March 1928
First used by Underground trains on 18 May 1941

'Hill on which a windmill stands' – recorded as Myllehill in 1547.

MONUMENT EC3
Circle, District
Opened as EASTCHEAP on 6 October 1884
Name changed to MONUMENT on 1 November 1884

The Monument is a tall column designed by Sir Christopher Wren in memory of the Great Fire of London in 1666. It is 202 feet high (61.57 metres), the exact distance between its position and the bakery in Pudding Lane where the fire started.

Wren originally wanted to put a statue of King Charles II on top, but the king objected to this, reasoning that he was not responsible for the fire! Charles II was, however, closely involved with dealing with the fire, and he took personal charge of pulling down houses to try to stop the spread of the flames.

Visitors can climb up the Monument at certain times, and there is an interesting view across the Thames. At one time, the Monument was a commanding landmark, but is now dwarfed by the huge modern buildings that surround it.

Within walking distance: London Bridge
                             The Monument
                             Southwark Cathedral

MOORGATE EC2
Circle, Hammersmith & City, Northern, Metropolitan
Opened as MOORGATE STREET on 23 December 1865
Name changed to simply MOORGATE on 24 October 1924
Northern Line opened as MOORGATE on 25 February 1900

In medieval times a moor gate led out to the moors and fens beyond the city of London. Originally it was a postern gate built in 1415 in the old city wall but was enlarged over the years. The height of the gateway was raised so that the London Trained Bands, an early form of Militia, could march through with their pikes held upright.

The gate was finally demolished in 1762, and the street, named Moorgate, was constructed in the 1840s.

Within walking distance: The Museum of London

MOOR PARK ESSEX
Metropolitan
Opened as SANDY LODGE on 9 May 1910
Name changed to MOOR PARK & SANDY LODGE on 18 October 1923
Finally changed to MOOR PARK on 25 September 1950

This station was opened in 1910 with the name Sandy Lodge. In 1923 the name was changed to Moor Park and Sandy Lodge – and then in 1950 it became simply Moor Park.

The original name, Sandy Lodge, is the name of a nearby golf course. Moor Park is an open public park near the golf course. But the name la More is recorded as early as *c.*1180.

MORDEN SURREY
Northern
Opened on 13 September 1926

'Morden' derives from two Old English words: *mor*, meaning 'marsh' and *dun*, 'hill'. It means a hill surrounded by marshy land.

The original Moor Gate, one of six gates in the city wall, demolished in 1762. Today's underground station preserves its memory.

MORNINGTON CRESCENT NW1
Northern
Opened on 22 June 1907
Closed on 23 October 1992
Re-opened on 27 April 1998

The imposing crescent of dwelling houses that is Mornington Crescent is named after Richard Wellesley, Earl of Mornington, the eldest brother of the Duke of Wellington. He served as foreign secretary from 1809–12. He was appointed lord lieutenant of Ireland in 1821, when the crescent was being built. The Underground station takes its name from this crescent.

MUDCHUTE E14
Docklands
Opened on 31 August 1987
Re-sited on 20 November 1999

This station is named after the nearby Mudchute Park and Farm. This was originally a piece of derelict land created in the nineteenth century from the spoil from the construction of Millwall Dock.

Since the late twentieth century this area has been developed into a remarkable educational and leisure facility, with the Mudchute Equestrian Centre, a café, a shop, an education centre and a large variety of farm animals to see: pigs, cows, goats, sheep, ducks, geese and even llamas.

NEASDEN NW10
Jubilee
Opened as KINGSBURY & NEASDEN on 2 August 1880
Named changed to NEASDEN & KINGSBURY on 1 January 1910
Finally changed to NEASDEN on 1 January 1932

Literally, this name, which is Saxon in origin, means 'nose-shaped hill', '*nese dun*'.

NEWBURY PARK ESSEX
Central
Opened by the Great Eastern Railway on 1 May 1903
First used by Underground trains on 14 December 1947

'The new manor house at the park' – 'new', however, is a relative term, as the name was first recorded in the middle of the fourteenth century. Newbury is derived from two Old English words: *niwe burh*.

NEW CROSS SE14
East London　(see NEW CROSS GATE)
Opened in October 1850
First used by Underground trains on 1 October 1884

NEW CROSS GATE SE14
East London
Opened as NEW CROSS on 5 June 1839
First used by Underground trains on 1 October 1884
Name changed to NEW CROSS GATE in 1923

The 'cross' referred to is the junction of the road to Dartford and the Old Kent Road.

NORTH ACTON NW10
Central　(see ACTON TOWN)
Opened on 5 November 1923

NORTH EALING W5
Piccadilly　(see EALING)
Opened on 23 June 1903

NORTHFIELDS W13
Piccadilly
Opened as NORTHFIELD HALT on 16 April 1908
Name changed to NORTHFIELDS & LITTLE EALING on 11 December 1911
Finally re-sited further east as NORTHFIELDS on 19 May 1932

The name goes back to the fifteenth century and is self–explanatory – the 'fields in the north'.

'TUBE' BABY!

In the 1920s, a baby girl was born on the Bakerloo Line. She was given the name Thelma Ursula Beatrice Eleanor – giving her the initials TUBE – an unforgettable reminder of her link with the London Underground!

NORTH GREENWICH SE10
Jubilee (see GREENWICH)
Opened on 14 May 1999

NORTH HARROW MIDDLESEX
Metropolitan (see HARROW)
Opened on 22 March 1915

NORTHOLT MIDDLESEX
Central
Opened on 21 November 1948

'Northern *halhs*'. The meaning of the Saxon word *halh* is not entirely clear. It could mean a corner, a secret place, a cave, recess, or some sort of 'nook'. The name of Southall in Middlesex is similarly derived – the 'Southern *halhs*'.

NORTH WEALD ESSEX
Formerly Central – now Epping Ongar Railway
Opened by the Eastern Counties/Great Eastern Railway in 1865
Central Line extended to use this station in 1949
Closed on 30 September 1994

Triumphantly re-opened on 10 October 2004 by the Epping Ongar Railway – the situation throughout the past half-century is so complicated that it cannot be described here. Those interested in following the historical details should consult the official website of the Epping Ongar Railway Volunteer Society (www.eorailway.co.uk) or Wikipedia.

   The Saxon word *weald* meant 'woodland'. Here, the name refers to Epping Forest.

NORTH WEMBLEY ESSEX
Bakerloo   (see WEMBLEY)
Opened as WEMBLEY CENTRAL by the London & North Western Railway
   on 15 June 1912
First used by Underground trains on 16 April 1917

NORTHWICK PARK MIDDLESEX
Metropolitan
Opened as NORTHWICK PARK & KENTON on 28 June 1923
Named changed to NORTHWICK PARK on 15 March 1937

Named after the Northwick family, who owned the manor of Harrow in the late eighteenth century. Today Northwick Park is the home of a popular and prestigious golf course.

NORTHWOOD ESSEX
Metropolitan   (see NORTHWOOD HILLS)
Opened on 1 September 1887

NORTHWOOD HILLS ESSEX
Metropolitan
Opened on 13 November 1933

Self-explanatory – the 'northern wood' – in this case the woodland
north of Ruislip. The arrival of the Metropolitan Line gave an
immediate boost to building development, and as a result of
this, the area soon lost most of its woodland. The 'hills' are also
self-explanatory, referring to high ground nearby.

NOTTING HILL GATE W11
Central, Circle, District
Opened on 1 October 1868

The 'gate' in this name is a reminder that here once was a turnpike
gate, built in the eighteenth century by the Uxbridge Turnpike
Trust. The gate was removed in 1864, just four years before the
Underground station opened.

'Notting' may derive from a family surname, the Knottings, in
which case the name would mean 'hill belonging to the Knotting
family'. As long ago as 1358 it was recorded as Knottynghull, and
in 1376 it appears as Knottyngwode. It has been suggested that the
family may have had a connection with the Bedfordshire village
of Knotting.

Within walking distance: Portobello Road Market

OAKWOOD N14
Piccadilly
Opened as ENFIELD WEST on 13 March 1933
Name changed to ENFIELD WEST (OAKWOOD) on 3 May 1934
Finally became simply OAKWOOD on 1 September 1946

The 'oak wood' referred to was once a part of Enfield Chase. The
first syllable of 'Enfield' derives from the name of a Saxon landowner
here – so 'Enfield' means 'Eana's clearing'.

Notting Hill in 1750 – very different from the scene of the Notting Hill festivals in the twenty-first century.

Notting Barn Farm in 1830, near today's Notting Hill Gate underground station.

OLD STREET EC1
Northern
Opened on 17 November 1901

When the Saxons came here, the Roman road out of London leading to Colchester was already several centuries old. According to John Stow, the sixteenth-century historian of London, Old Street got its name 'for that it was the old highway from Aldersgate for the north east parts of England, before Bishopsgate was built'. The name was given further significance when this Underground station opened in 1901.

OSTERLEY MIDDLESEX
Piccadilly
Opened as OSTERLEY & SPRING GROVE on 1 May 1883
Name changed and station re-sited on 25 March 1934

'Woodland clearing with a sheepfold' – the name derives from two Old English words, *eowestre* and *leah*.

OVAL SE11
Northern
Opened on 18 December 1890

Kennington Oval was opened for cricket in 1845. Formerly, it had been a part of a market garden, and before that it had been part of a site on which a royal residence had been built (see KENNINGTON). The first Test Match in England against Australia was played here in 1880 – happily, England won by five wickets.

The name is derived from the Latin word *ovum*, meaning 'egg', so it simply means 'egg-shaped'. Perhaps this is appropriate for those cricketers who are 'out for a duck' – which is short for a 'duck's egg' the shape of which is 0, or nothing!

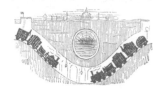

OXFORD CIRCUS WI
Bakerloo, Central, Victoria
Opened on 30 July 1900

Oxford Street was once known as Tyburn Road, and the notorious Tyburn gallows stood at its western end, near where Marble Arch stands today. The reason for its present name, which became established in the early eighteenth century, is that much of the land to the north of it was bought by Edward Harley, 2nd Earl of Oxford.

Oxford 'Circus' was a part of John Nash's circular design at the place where his New Street (later to be known as Regent Street) crossed the much older Oxford Street.

The road we now know as Oxford Street has existed in one form or another possibly from as early as Roman times.

Within walking distance: Oxford Street shops
                             Soho

PADDINGTON W2
Bakerloo, Circle, District, Hammersmith & City
Opened as PADDINGTON (BISHOP'S ROAD) by the Hammersmith & City
*   Line on 10 January 1863*
Name changed to PADDINGTON on this line on 10 September 1933
Opened as PADDINGTON (PRAED STREET) by the Circle Line on
*   1 October 1868*
Name changed to PADDINGTON on this line on 11 July 1948
Opened as PADDINGTON by the Bakerloo Line on 1 December 1913

The name Paddington is typical of so many Saxon names. Padda was the name of the Saxon leader who settled here; *ingas* meant 'family' or 'followers' of Padda; and the ending *tun* simply tells us that this was their 'village'.

As an Underground station, Paddington was part of the very first stretch of the Metropolitan Line, which opened in 1863 with Paddington as the western terminus of the world's first underground system.

As for the main-line railway station, Paddington began its life as a wooden structure, and opened as early as 1838 – the year of Queen Victoria's coronation. Queen Victoria herself arrived here on her

Paddington village church shown as it was in 1750 and then, after 'improve-ments', as it was in 1805.

very first railway journey – from Slough – in 1842. She had been somewhat alarmed at the speed, which averaged 44 miles per hour. ('Not so fast next time, Mr Conductor' admonished Prince Albert!)

PADDINGTON BEAR

Paddington Bear, the star of Michael Bond's popular children's stories, was named after Paddington Station. The author and his wife were living nearby when he bought a small teddy bear. The name was an inspired choice! A large Paddington Bear statue is now on permanent view in the main-line station's entrance hall.

It is interesting to imagine what Padda, the Old Saxon chief, would think if he could return and see his ursine namesake!

PARK ROYAL NW10
Piccadilly
Opened as PARK ROYAL & TWYFORD ABBEY on 23 June 1903
Name changed and the station re-sited on 6 July 1931

Although this name may sound ancient and connected with royalty, in fact it is relatively recent. In the late nineteenth century the Royal Agricultural Society obtained a large site here for a permanent exhibition – a 'park' for themselves. It was a scheme that never succeeded, and the area became used for industry. The name, Park Royal, however, remained, and when the Underground station was opened in 1903 it was originally named Park Royal & Twyford Abbey.

PARSONS GREEN SW6
District
Opened on 1 March 1880

A parsonage or rectory, which stood here for centuries, provides the name for this area – it was 'the village green standing by the parson's house'. The parsonage itself was first mentioned in 1391 and was finally demolished in 1882.

PERIVALE MIDDLESEX
Central
Opened as PERIVALE HALT by the Great Western Railway on 2 May 1904
First used by Underground trains on 30 June 1947

'Pear tree valley'. Before the sixteenth century this hamlet was called Little Greenford or Greenford Parva, meaning 'the small village by the green ford'. The next station along the Central Line is Greenford – which is named after Greenford Magna – 'the *large* village by the green ford'.

PICCADILLY CIRCUS W1
Bakerloo, Piccadilly
Opened on 10 March 1906

In the early seventeenth century, a London tailor called Robert Baker made a fortune for himself by selling 'picadils' – a kind of wide stiff collar that was fashionable at that time – from his shop in the Strand.

Out of the profits he bought lands to the north of what is now Piccadilly Circus, on which he built himself a large house. Londoners of the time promptly nicknamed this mansion 'Piccadilly Hall'.

The name Piccadilly has remained attached to this part of London ever since and became even better known when Piccadilly Circus was formed in 1819, at the intersection of Piccadilly with John Nash's newly constructed Regent Street.

Piccadilly Circus as it was in 1875 – just a decade or so after the first Underground trains began to run.

Within walking distance: Burlington House and Burlington Arcade
Piccadilly Circus and the 'Eros' statue
Regent Street
St James's Piccadilly
Soho

EROS AT PICCADILLY

Everyone knows the statue of 'Eros' in the middle of Piccadilly Circus – and everyone knows that Eros is the Greek God of sexual love.

However, when the sculptor Sir Alfred Gilbert (1854–1934), created the statue and designed the fountain, he meant it to represent the Angel of Christian Charity. It was intended to be a memorial to the great public benefactor, Anthony Ashley Cooper, 7th Earl of Shaftesbury (1801–85), who campaigned to reform factories, reduce working hours, and prohibit underground employment of women and children in coal mines.

The statue, made of aluminium, was unveiled in 1893, and the nickname 'Eros' instantly became universal – though who first thought of it will never be known.

PIMLICO SW1
Victoria
Opened on 14 September 1972

The station name Pimlico is something of a mystery. It may be derived from the name of an innkeeper, Ben Pimlico, who lived in Hoxton in the late sixteenth century and was famous for his 'nut-brown ale'. Somehow his name became that of his hostelry and then of the surrounding area. An early version of the word is recorded in 1630 as Pimplico, referring to what was then an almost uninhabited district in Westminster.

Other suggested explanations of 'Pimlico' are that it was the name of some long-forgotten drink, or – perhaps far-fetched – that it is linked with the Pamlico tribe of native Americans, who used to export timber to England in the seventeenth century.

This word has been puzzled over for several centuries.

PINNER MIDDLESEX
Metropolitan
Opened on 25 May 1885

'Pynn's home by the river bank'. Pynn was a Saxon name, and *ora* is
Old English for a riverbank. Interestingly, the *ora* part of the name
is also found in 'Windsor' – which means 'the river bank where the
windlass is' – a curious derivation for the name of the royal house
of Windsor.

PLAISTOW E13
District, Hammersmith & City
Opened by the London, Tilbury & Southend Railway on 31 March 1858
First used by Underground trains on 2 June 1902

The Old English word *plegstow* means 'playground'. This area was a
place of recreation, and the name is first recorded here as long ago
as 1414 as Playstowe. There are similar place names in other parts of
England, all meaning 'sports area'.

PONTOON DOCK E16
Docklands
Opened on 2 December 2005

Pontoon Dock Station was opened in December 2005 on the King
George V branch of the Docklands Light Railway, between West
Silverton and London City. The word 'pontoon' – here meaning the
floating gate of a dock – is derived from the Latin word *ponto*, 'a punt'.

POPLAR E14
Docklands
Opened on 31 August 1987

The land in this area is very marshy and suited to poplars, the rapidly
growing trees of the willow family, which give this district its name.
The word comes from the Old French word *poplier*, which in turn
was derived from the Latin *populus*, 'a poplar tree'.

POPLAR IN THE BLITZ

A girl in Poplar had a most embarrassing moment in the Blitz on London during the Second World War. She was having a bath when a bomb hit her house. The bomb blast shattered the house and the bath was turned upside down with the girl herself still inside it. Luckily, the bath provided the perfect shelter from the bricks and rubble dropping around her.

After the air raid, she was dug out, frightened, safe, wet and stark naked.

She was lucky. It was been calculated that more than 15,000 people were killed in the London Blitz, and over 3.5 million houses were damaged or destroyed.

PRESTON ROAD MIDDLESEX
Metropolitan
Opened as PRESTON ROAD HALT on 21 May 1908
Name changed to PRESTON ROAD and station re-sited on 22 November 1931

The 'Preston' part of this station name derives from two Old English words: *preosta* and *tun*, meaning 'homestead of the priests'. The name is very widespread, in fact there are more than forty place names in Britain consisting of or containing the word 'preston'.

PRINCE REGENT E16
Docklands
Opened on 28 March 1994

Named in memory of 'Prinny' – the Prince of Wales, son of King George III (reigned 1760–1820), who became Regent of Great Britain for nine years (1811–20) during the period when his father became so mentally ill that he was unable to undertake his royal duties. On the death of his father in 1820, the Prince Regent became crowned as King George IV and reigned until 1830.

PUDDING MILL LANE E15
Docklands
Opened on 15 January 1996

Pudding Mill Lane (E15) must not be confused with the Pudding Lane in the City of London (EC3) where the Great Fire of London started in 1666.

The word 'pudding', however, is common to both lanes, and it may come as a surprise to some to learn that in the Middle Ages – and later – 'pudding' referred to the guts and entrails of slaughtered animals. We still have a linguistic memory of this meaning in the name of 'black pudding' – which is made of dried blood.

'Pudding' had to be disposed of, and the rivers and tributaries of the Thames provided a convenient dumping place.

A windmill stood near here until the early nineteenth century, when it was demolished, but quite what the connection was between the 'pudding' and the 'mill' is unclear.

PUTNEY BRIDGE SW15
District
Opened as PUTNEY BRIDGE & FULHAM on 1 March 1880
Name changed to PUTNEY BRIDGE & HURLINGHAM on 1 September 1902
Finally became simply PUTNEY BRIDGE in 1932

A Saxon chieftain called Puttan is remembered in the name of Putney. Together with the Saxon word *hyp*, 'landing place', the name means 'Puttan's wharf'.

QUEENSBURY NW9
Jubilee
Opened on 16 December 1934

The name Queensbury has no historical roots. It was the winning suggestion in a competition run by an estate agent in the 1930s. The Underground station, opened in 1934, needed a name, and Queensbury appealed to the judges of the competition because it complemented the next station along this line – Kingsbury – which had opened two years earlier, in 1932.

QUEEN'S PARK NW6
Bakerloo
*Opened as QUEEN'S PARK (WEST KILBURN) by the London and North
    Western Railway on 2 June 1879*
*This new station was first used by Underground trains as QUEEN'S PARK on
    11 February 1915*

The park in this area after which the Underground station is named
was laid out by the Corporation of the City of London and opened
in 1887 to honour Queen Victoria in the year of her Golden Jubilee.

QUEENSWAY W2
Central
Opened as QUEEN'S ROAD on 30 July 1900
Name changed to QUEENSWAY on 1 September 1946

Queensway, the road on which this station is built, was once called
Black Lion Lane, named after a pub here called The Black Lion. This
road was renamed Queensway in honour of Queen Victoria shortly
after she came to the throne in 1837, for this was one of the roads
along which she rode as she left her home in Kensington Palace.

   The old name of the road is still remembered in Black Lion Gate,
which leads from Queensway into Kensington Gardens.

Within walking distance: Diana, Princess of Wales
                                 Memorial Fountain
                             Kensington Gardens and
                                 Peter Pan statue
                             Kensington Palace
                             Serpentine Gallery

RAVENSCOURT PARK W6
District
*Opened as SHAFTESBURY ROAD by the London & South Western Railway
    on 1 April 1873*
Name changed to RAVENSCOURT PARK on 1 March 1888
First used by Underground trains on 1 June 1877

'Ravenscourt' is a word with a curious history. In 1747, Thomas
Corbett, Secretary to the Admiralty, bought the manor here. Its name
was Paddenswick and it was an ancient manor house owned in the
fourteenth century by Alice Perrers, mistress of King Edward III
(reigned 1327–77).

Thomas Corbett was extremely proud of his name, and even had a
raven on his coat of arms, because *corbeau* is French for 'raven' and so
this was a kind of pun on his name 'Corbett'.

Just to make sure everyone was aware of the *corbeau*/Corbett
pun, he went to the length of changing the name of his house:
Paddenswick became Ravenscourt.

RAYNERS LANE MIDDLESEX
Metropolitan, Piccadilly
Opened as RAYNERS LANE HALT on 26 May 1906

This station is named after an old shepherd called Daniel Rayner,
who lived alone in a cottage near here until about 1905.

The Metropolitan Railway opened its station here in 1906 and
gave it the name Rayners Lane – thus giving this old shepherd a
permanent memorial.

REDBRIDGE ILFORD
Central
Opened on 14 December 1947

There used to be a red bridge here over the river Roding, which
was the boundary between Wanstead and Ilford. The bridge was
demolished in 1922, but the name hung about, and was adopted to
name the Underground station here when it opened twenty-five
years later, in 1947.

REGENT'S PARK NW1
Bakerloo
Opened on 10 March 1906

When King George III became incurably mad in 1810 it was necessary to replace him as king. His eldest son, the Prince of Wales, also a George, took over his duties and for nine years he ruled the country uniquely as 'Regent'.

These were momentous years for the development of London, and the Regent's energetic architect, John Nash, transformed the capital, giving us Regent's Park, Regent Street and the vastly enlarged Buckingham House, which became Buckingham Palace.

Regent's Park was originally known as Marylebone Park, and the well-forested land here was acquired by Henry VIII for use as a hunting area. John Nash planned its development as a town park during the Napoleonic wars, and by 1841 it was opened to the public.

Regent Street, originally known as New Street, was designed specially to run from Regent's Park to Carlton House, the Regent's home in the Mall (now demolished).

Within walking distance: London Zoo

RICHMOND SURREY
District
Opened by the London & South Western Railway on 27 July 1846
First used by District Underground trains on 1 June 1877

Henry VII (reigned 1485–1509) had been Earl of Richmond in Yorkshire before he defeated Richard III at the Battle of Bosworth Field and seized the throne.

When he became king he decided to rebuild the royal palace of Sheen for himself and to rename it Rychmonde – alluding to his former earldom. The Richmond here in Surrey, therefore, is a transplant from Yorkshire.

The name Richmond is pure Norman French – *Richemont*, or 'royal hill'. Originally it was the name of a village in Normandy, and when Count Alan of Brittany, a cousin of William the Conqueror, built his castle in Yorkshire, he gave it this name from Normandy. William the Conqueror created him Earl of Richmond.

106   *Why Do Shepherds Need a Bush?*

Other Richmonds in California, Indiana, New York City and the capital of Virginia show how popular this name has been.

RICKMANSWORTH HERTFORDSHIRE
Metropolitan
Opened on 1 September 1887

The Old English word *worth* means 'homestead'. 'Rickmansworth' is 'Ricmar's homestead'.

RODING VALLEY ESSEX
Central
Opened by the London & North Eastern Railway on 3 February 1936
First used by Underground trains on 21 November 1948

The river Roding used to be called the river Hyle, which gave Ilford its name ('ford on the Hyle').

Roding itself derived its name from the fact that it was once the dwelling of the *ing*, or 'family', of a Saxon leader who had a name something like 'Hroda'.

There are no fewer than nine 'Roding' villages lying on or near this river: Abbess Roding, Aythorpe Roding, Barwick Roding, Beauchamp Roding, Berners Roding, High Roding, Leaden Roding, Margaret Roding and White Roding. All these have interesting derivations, for example, 'Leaden' Roding is so named because of the costly leaden roof that its church possessed.

ROTHERHITHE SE16
East London
Opened by the East London Railway on 7 December 1869
Metropolitan and District Lines began to use this station on 1 October 1884
Metropolitan Line closed on 31 July 1905
District Line closed on 2 December 1906
Metropolitan Line resumed on 31 March 1913

There are a number of place names ending in *hythe*, which is an Old English word for a 'landing place'.

The first part of these names usually denotes what sort of commodity was handled at that particular landing place – in this case it was cattle, the name coming directly from another Old English word – *rother*.

Interestingly, a famous name in London contains a hidden form of the Old English *hythe* – Lambeth – which derives from the fact that it was a 'lambs' *hythe*', or a place where lambs were the main item which was traded.

ROYAL ALBERT E16
Docklands
Opened on 28 March 1994

Named after the Royal Albert Dock, opened in 1880 and one of the Royal Group of Docks (the other two are the Royal Victoria (1855) and the King George V (1921)).

The Royal Albert Dock itself was named after Prince Albert (1819–61), Consort of Queen Victoria.

The Royal Albert Dock and the Royal Victoria Dock lie end to end, separated by the Connaught Bridge, and together they contain 175 acres of water and provide 7 miles of quay. Sadly, they are hardly in use today.

ROYAL OAK W2
Hammersmith & City
Opened on 30 October 1871

Royal Oak is named after an old inn that once stood near where Paddington Station is now situated. The inn no longer exists, but the Underground station, opened in 1871, preserves its name.

Royal Oak pubs exist throughout the British Isles, named after the famous oak tree in which King Charles II hid after his defeat at the Battle of Worcester in 1651. He hid in this tree while the soldiers of Cromwell's army were scouring the woods looking for him. He managed to evade them and a few weeks later escaped to France, where he remained in exile until he was recalled to be crowned in 1660.

ROYAL VICTORIA E16
Docklands
Opened on 28 March 1994

Named after the Royal Victoria Dock, opened in 1855. The first to be constructed of the group of three 'Royal' docks. (See ROYAL ALBERT)

RUISLIP MIDDLESEX
Metropolitan, Piccadilly
Opened on 4 July 1904

'Ruislip' is Old English, meaning 'the wet place where the rushes grow'. The name is derived from two words: *rysc*, meaning 'rush', and *slaep*, meaning 'wet place'.

   An alternative explanation of the second part of this name is that it derives from *hlype*, meaning 'leap'. If this is so, it would refer to a point on the river where, if you were athletic enough, you could 'leap' across it – or perhaps your horse could make the jump across.

RUISLIP GARDENS MIDDLESEX
Central   (see RUISLIP)
Opened on 21 November 1948

RUISLIP MANOR MIDDLESEX
Central   (see RUISLIP)
Opened on 5 August 1912

Ruislip Manor takes its name from a Manor Farm, which has been in this area since the Middle Ages.

RUSSELL SQUARE WC1
Piccadilly
Opened on 15 December 1906

Russell Square is built on land belonging to the Russells – Russell is the family name of the Dukes of Bedford. There are over seventy Bedford/Russell place names in this area of London, showing just how influential this family was in the history of London's development.

Russell Square is the largest of all London's squares, and it was laid out in 1800 by Humphrey Repton (1752–1818) the famous landscape gardener. The Underground station was opened in 1906.

Within walking distance: The British Museum
    The Charles Dickens Museum

ST JAMES'S PARK W1
Circle, District
Opened on 24 December 1868

St James's Park derives its name from St James's Hospital for leper women, which stood here long before King Henry VIII rebuilt it as St James's Palace after he acquired it in 1532.

According to the sixteenth-century historian John Stow, there was an old hospital here even before the Norman Conquest. It was dedicated to St James the Less because he is the patron saint of lepers.

St James's Palace is still a royal residence, and all foreign ambassadors are still, even today, accredited to the Court of St James. It is from a balcony of this palace that the formal announcement of the death of a sovereign is made – together with the proclamation of the successor: 'The King [Queen] is dead. Long live the King!'

The old leper women would have been astonished if they had known that St James would become the name of a park and then of an Underground station!

Within walking distance: Buckingham Palace
    Houses of Parliament and Big Ben
    Jewel Tower
    Queen's Gallery
    Royal Mews
    Westminster Abbey

ST JOHN'S WOOD NW8
Jubilee

An earlier station of this name was opened by the Metropolitan Line on
*   13 April 1868*
It was replaced by a new station, which opened on the Bakerloo Line on
*   20 November 1939*
This was transferred to the Jubilee Line in 1979

This area was formerly owned by the Knights Templar (see TEMPLE), but when the Knights Templar were disbanded in 1312, the land was given to the Knights of St John of Jerusalem. It was thickly wooded throughout the Middle Ages – hence 'St John's Wood'.

The name began in this manner and has remained ever since, although since the Reformation there have been many owners and the land has been divided into separate estates.

ST PANCRAS (KING'S CROSS ST PANCRAS) NW1
Circle, Hammersmith & City, Northern, Victoria
(see KING'S CROSS ST PANCRAS)

For most people, St Pancras is simply a railway station, and it takes an effort of will to remember that the old church of St Pancras, in whose parish the station is built and which gave its name to the station, is dedicated to a fourteen-year-old Roman boy called Pancratius. According to tradition he was converted to Christianity and was put to death for his faith by the Emperor Diocletian in the year 304.

Although he is scarcely remembered today, it is worth noting that when St Augustine brought Christianity to Kent in the year 597, the very first church he consecrated at Canterbury was dedicated to St Pancras.

At St Pancras Old Church in London, a Saxon altar was found, dating from about 600. This means that it is one of the oldest Christian sites in Britain.

It is an odd quirk of history that it took over fifteen centuries and the invention of the railway to make the name of this murdered Roman teenager an everyday household word for thousands of modern commuters.

The village church of St Pancras in 1820.

The little Fleet River meandering gently near St Pancras in 1825. Fleet Street gets its name from this little stream.

ST PAUL'S EC4
Central
Opened as POST OFFICE on 30 July 1900
Name changed to ST PAUL'S on 1 February 1937

Obviously, this station is named after the great cathedral that stands nearby. However, it is interesting to note that the building we see today, designed by Sir Christopher Wren, is the fifth St Paul's to occupy this site – and even before the first cathedral, there had been a Roman Temple to Diana on this spot.

Within walking distance: Globe Theatre
    Guildhall
    Museum of London
    Paternoster Square (incorporating the
      old Temple Bar)
    St Martin-within-Ludgate
    St Paul's Cathedral

The seven trees planted in memory of seven sisters – as seen in 1830.

THE FIVE ST PAUL'S CATHEDRALS

The first St Paul's Cathedral was built in 604 by Ethelbert, the Saxon King of Kent, who was the first Christian king in England. It was destroyed by fire.

The second St Paul's Cathedral was built between 675 and 685 by Erconwald, the fourth Bishop of London. The Vikings destroyed this building in 961.

A third St Paul's Cathedral was built shortly afterwards, but this was also destroyed by fire in 1087.

The fourth St Paul's Cathedral, which most people know as 'Old St Paul's', was built by Maurice, Bishop of London and Chaplain to William the Conqueror. This beautiful building was one of the largest cathedrals ever built. Its spire was the tallest of any church in the world – 520 feet (158.5 metres). In comparison, Salisbury Cathedral's spire is 404 feet high (121.92 metres), and the London Telecom Tower is 580 feet high (176.78 metres) – only 60 feet more (18.29 metres).

Old St Paul's was destroyed by the Great Fire of London in 1666. The present cathedral, built by Sir Christopher Wren, was begun in 1675 and completed in 1710.

Wren was seventy-eight years old when the cathedral was completed, so his son laid the last stone of all in the lantern at the top.

SEVEN SISTERS N7
Victoria
Opened on 1 September 1968

A story is told that there was once in this area a family of seven sisters, who, when they grew up and decided to go their various ways, planted seven elm trees outside a pub in Tottenham, as a sort of memorial to themselves. Who they were is now forgotten, but their sisterly enterprise has given us the name of the road and also of this Underground station.

SHADWELL E1
Docklands
Opened on 31 August 1987

Shadwell is derived from two words, meaning 'shallow well' or 'shallow stream'.

SHEPHERD'S BUSH W12
Central
Opened on 30 July 1900

In earlier times this area had the picturesque name of Gagglegoose Green. The present name of Shepherd's Bush is another reminder that until comparatively recently many parts of London were still completely rural.

This name derives from the widespread practice among shepherds of clipping and trimming a suitable tree or bush into a sort of upright shelter which was lined with straw so that they could stand, leaning back, to watch their sheep in comfort.

There used to be 'shepherd's bushes' throughout the country, but nowadays the name of this area near West Kensington is virtually the only reminder of this ancient custom.

Within walking distance: Westfield Shopping Centre, opened in
                             2008, Europe's largest in-town
                             shopping centre.

'... A BEAUTIFUL PIECE OF TOPIARY WORK'

From an article in *The Morning Post*, 1910

There are in many parts of the country ... shepherd's bushes still in existence, and as they are invariably situated on rolling downs and commons in out-of-the-way haunts of solitude, a short description may not be out of place.

Imagine, then, a stiff thorn-bush with the sharp and slender leaf-stems starting about three feet from the ground. Instead of the bush being left to grow in the ordinary way, all the inner wood has been cut out until an oval cup has been formed by the sprouting outer branches growing densely together to a thickness of about eighteen inches, while the trunk of the bush forms at its top a platform within and a step without.

On the top of this platform are placed and replaced, as required, bundles of clean wheaten straw, so that with a sack thrown over the inside of the cup to shield him from the prickles the shepherd can stand up with his arms resting on the edges of the bowl and look around him far and wide, watching the movements of his flock.

... When such a bush is kept judiciously clipped and trimmed it forms an effective, artistic, and even beautiful piece of topiary work, especially in the months of May and early June, when the hawthorn is in full bloom.

SHEPHERD'S BUSH MARKET W12
Hammersmith & City   (see SHEPHERD'S BUSH)
Opened as SHEPHERD'S BUSH on 1 April 1914
Changed to SHEPHERD'S BUSH MARKET in 2008

SHOREDITCH N1
East London Section (Limited service)
Opened by the East London Railway on 10 April 1876
First used by Underground trains on 31 March 1913

It has been thought that this refers to a ditch near the shore of the Thames, but this is somewhat unlikely, as the Thames is quite a distance from here. The first record of the name appears in a manuscript of 1148, and is given as Scoredich, so it is much more likely to derive from a personal name, being the 'ditch of Sceorf' or 'Scorre'.

Shoreditch Station has been described as 'possibly the least known Underground station in Inner London'.

SLOANE SQUARE SW1
Circle, District
Opened on 24 December 1868

Named after one of the most remarkable men to have lived in London, Sir Hans Sloane (1660–1753). He was born in Ireland, the son of an Ulster Scot, and arrived in London when he was nineteen to study medicine and natural history. After a varied life of study and travel he became President of the College of Physicians, Physician General to the Army and, in 1727, he was appointed Royal Physician. He succeeded Sir Isaac Newton as President of the Royal Society.

He wrote many books on medicine and natural history, and when he died, aged ninety-two, his personal museum and his collection of 50,000 books and 3,560 manuscripts formed the beginning of the British Museum.

He was Lord of the Manor of Chelsea, and this is why in that area there are so many roads named after him: Sloane Square, Sloane Street, Sloane Avenue, Sloane Court, Sloane Gardens, Sloane Terrace – as well as Hans Crescent, Hans Place, Hans Street, Hans Road and, of course, Sloane Square Underground Station.

Within walking distance: National Army Museum

SNARESBROOK E11
Central
Opened as SNAKESBROOK & WANSTEAD by the Eastern Counties
*   Railway on 22 August 1856*
First used by Underground trains and name changed to SNARESBROOK on
*   14 December 1947*

'The brook where snares and traps are laid.'

SOUTH EALING W5
Piccadilly   (see EALING)
Opened on 1 May 1883

SOUTHFIELDS SW18
District
Opened on 3 June 1889

Originally this was the site of the 'south fields' of a former manor house, Durnsford Manor.

SOUTHGATE N14
Piccadilly
Opened on 13 March 1933

Southgate station is named after the hamlet that grew up by this entrance to Enfield Chase. It is recorded as Suthgate in 1370, and Le South Gate in 1608. Lord Lawrence, Viceroy of India 1863–69, lived at Southgate House – which later became Minchenden School (now closed).

SOUTH HARROW ESSEX
Piccadilly   (see HARROW & WEALDSTONE)
Opened on 28 June 1903
Re-sited on 5 July 1935

SOUTH KENSINGTON SW7
Circle, District, Piccadilly   (see KENSINGTON (OLYMPIA))
Opened on 24 December 1868

Within walking distance: Albert Memorial and Royal Albert Hall
                                Brompton Oratory
                                Hyde Park
                                Kensington Gardens, Diana Memorial,
                                Peter Pan Statue, Serpentine

Kensington Palace
Natural History Museum
Royal College of Music
Science Museum
Victoria and Albert Museum

SOUTH KENTON MIDDLESEX
Bakerloo
Opened on 3 July 1933

'The farm or homestead belonging to Cœna' – who was a
Saxon chieftain.

SOUTH QUAY E14
Docklands
Opened on 31 August 1987

The name of this station is clearly a reference to a quay in the
docklands area. This Docklands station is situated between Heron
Quays and Crossharbour, but it is scheduled to close and be relocated
– its proposed name is Millennium Quarter, a reference to the time
of the redevelopment of the whole dockland area.

SOUTH RUISLIP MIDDLESEX
Central   (see RUISLIP)
Opened by the Great Western Railway and Great Central Railway as
*   NORTHOLT JUNCTION on 1 May 1908*
Name changed to SOUTH RUISLIP & NORTHOLD JUNCTION on
*   12 September 1932*
Changed again to SOUTH RUISLIP on 30 June 1947

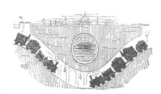

SOUTHWARK SE1
Jubilee
Opened on 20 November 1999

'Buildings on the south bank' or 'southern defensive work'. In early centuries this part of London, south of the Thames and opposite the City, obviously needed to be well fortified in order to deter possible invaders who wished to cross the river at this point.

Within walking distance: Shakespeare's Globe Theatre
                                Tate Modern

SOUTH WIMBLEDON SW19
Northern   (see WIMBLEDON)
Opened on 13 September 1926

SOUTH WOODFORD E18
Central   (see WOODFORD)
Opened by the Eastern Counties Railway as GEORGE LANE on
*   22 August 1856*
Name changed to SOUTH WOODFORD (GEORGE LANE) on 5 July 1937
First used by Underground trains on 14 December 1947
Name finally changed to SOUTH WOODFORD in 1950

STAMFORD BROOK W6
District
Opened on 1 February 1912

'Brook with the stony ford'. The 'ford' itself was on the Great West Road and the 'brook' was one of the tributaries of the Thames, formed by three streams. Stamford Brook itself was turned into a sewer by the end of the nineteenth century. The name of this Underground station is an almost subliminal reminder that the brook ever existed.

STANMORE MIDDLESEX
Jubilee
Opened on 10 December 1932

The name of this station, the last one at the northern end of the
Jubilee Line, means 'stony mere', referring to the 'mere', or pond, on
Stanmore Common, which is locally known as 'Caesar's Pond'.

If legend is to be believed, it was here that the ancient British
leader, Cassivellaunus, and his tribe, the Catuvellauni, fought a
battle with Julius Caesar in 54 BC. There used to be an obelisk on
Stanmore Common, erected in 1750, to commemorate the event,
but this is now in the grounds of the National Orthopaedic Hospital.

Another local tradition holds that it was near here, on Stanmore
Common, that Boudicca (Boadicea) was finally defeated by the
Romans in AD 61 after her ferocious attack on London.

STEPNEY GREEN E1
District, Hammersmith & City
Opened by the Whitechapel and Bow Railway on 23 June 1902
District had begun to use the line three weeks earlier
First used by Metropolitan Line (Hammersmith & City) on 30 March 1936

The 'Stepney' part of this name means 'Stebba's landing-place' – a
Thames-side settlement of a Saxon leader. It can be compared with
Putney. (See PUTNEY)

STOCKWELL SW9
Northern, Victoria
Opened on 18 December 1890

This name was first recorded in 1197, meaning 'the well or spring by
the tree stump'.

STONEBRIDGE PARK NW10
Bakerloo
Opened by the London & North Western Railway on 15 June 1912
First used by Underground trains on 16 April 1917

A stone bridge over the river Brent gave its name to a former farm here, Stonebridge Farm. The farm disappeared when housing development took place in this area in the 1870s and 1880s. This housing development was given the name Stonebridge Park Estate. The Underground station on the Bakerloo Line took up the name when it opened here in 1917.

STRATFORD E15
Central, Docklands, Jubilee
Opened by the Eastern Counties Railway on 20 June 1839
First used by Underground trains on 4 December 1946

The old Roman road (street) to Colchester crossed the river Lea at this spot, where there was a somewhat deep and dangerous ford. It is the 'street ford'. A bridge was ultimately built to avoid the necessity of getting wet braving the ford. (See BOW ROAD)

SUDBURY HILL MIDDLESEX
Piccadilly   (see SUDBURY TOWN)
Opened on 28 June 1903

SUDBURY TOWN MIDDLESEX
Piccadilly
Opened on 28 June 1903

Sudbury means 'Southern manor'.

SURREY QUAYS SE16
East London
Opened as DEPTFORD ROAD by the East London Railway on
*   7 December 1869*
First used by Underground trains on 1 October 1884
Name changed to SURREY DOCKS on 17 July 1911
After major reconstruction, the name was changed again to SURREY QUAYS
*   on 24 October 1989*

The present name, Surrey Quays, was given to this station to coincide with the opening of a nearby shopping centre, which had been given this name.

SWISS COTTAGE NW3
Jubilee
Opened by the Metropolitan Railway on 13 April 1868
That station closed on 18 August 1940 and was replaced by another station
of the same name on the Bakerloo Line, opening on 20 November 1939
This finally became a part of the Jubilee Line on 1 May 1979

When Finchley Road was first constructed in 1826, a toll gate was established at the southern end to help pay for it, and one of the first buildings to grow up near it on the new road was a picturesque tavern designed in the style of a Swiss alpine chalet.

Swiss Tavern, as it was then known (later Swiss Cottage) has given its name to the station of the Jubilee Line and the whole surrounding area.

The original Swiss Cottage as it was at the beginning of the nineteenth century.

TEMPLE EC4
Circle, District (closed Sundays)
Opened on 30 May 1870

The name 'temple' is found in many places around the meeting point of Fleet Street and the Strand: Temple Bar, Temple Avenue, Middle Temple Lane and of course Temple Church itself, after which Temple Underground Station is named.

The Temple Church has a history going back more than 800 years – see below.

Within walking distance:	Courtauld Gallery (Somerset House)
	Dr Johnson's House
	Royal Courts of Justice
	St Dunstan-in-the-West
	St Clement Dane
	Strand
	The Temple and the Inns of Court
	Temple Bar Monument

LONDON'S TEMPLE CHURCH...

In 1118, nine French knights formed the beginning of an Order of Chivalry to protect pilgrims on their way to the Holy Land. They became known as Templars, or Knights Templar, because they had their headquarters in Jerusalem on the site of the old Temple of Solomon.

The Templars quickly grew in number and influence, spreading throughout Europe. In England they built a great house and a round church on the banks of the Thames in 1185, and called this church the New Temple. Its circular shape is believed to have been modelled on the Church of the Holy Sepulchre at Jerusalem, built by Constantine over the reputed tomb of Christ. There are five such circular churches in England, including the well-known Round Church in Cambridge.

…AND LONDON'S TEMPLE BAR

Temple Bar, near the Temple Church, marks the boundary between the City of London and the City of Westminster. It sometimes comes as a surprise to visitors to find that today's 'London' consists of *two* cities.

Nowadays, in the middle of Fleet Street, this boundary between the two cities is marked by the Griffin Pillar, erected in 1880. In the Middle Ages there was simply a chain stretched between wooden posts; later, there was a city gate with a prison on top and then, after the Great Fire of London, Sir Christopher Wren rebuilt it and stretched his beautiful Temple Bar across the Strand.

With increasing traffic, Wren's Temple Bar proved to be far too narrow, so it was pulled down in 1870 – the very year in which this Underground station – then called The Temple – was opened. Over the years, it has become, simply, 'Temple'.

Throughout the twentieth century Temple Bar was virtually forgotten by most people. It had been taken down and re-erected in the grounds of Theobald's – a large country house in Hertfordshire.

Triumphantly, however, Temple Bar was carefully taken down again in the early twenty-first century and *re*-re-erected as a pedestrian gateway to the redeveloped Paternoster Square, adjacent to St Paul's Cathedral. It was officially opened in November 2004 by the Mayor of London – a remarkable moment in London's architectural history.

THEYDON BOIS ESSEX
Central

Opened by the Great Eastern Railway as THEYDON on 24 April 1865
Name changed to THEYDON BOIS on 1 December 1865
First used by Underground trains on 25 September 1949

Theydon is an Old English word meaning 'valley where thatch can be obtained' and *Bois* is the French word for a wood.

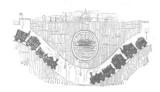

Temple Bar in its original position in Fleet Street in the early eighteenth century. Note the three poles sticking up into the air – they hold aloft the heads of beheaded criminals.

TOOTING BEC SW12
Northern
Opened as TRINITY ROAD on 13 September 1926
Name changed to TOOTING BEC on 1 October 1950

The 'Tooting' part of this station name is Saxon, and means 'place where Tota's followers live' and 'Bec' refers to the fact that in medieval times the land here was owned by the Benedictine Abbey of St Mary of Bec in Normandy.

TOOTING BROADWAY SW12
Northern   (see TOOTING BEC)
Opened on 13 September 1926

The Broadway was formerly a large open space near the station – it is now just a small triangular area.

TOTTENHAM COURT ROAD N17
Central, Northern
Opened by the Central London Railway on 30 July 1900
An adjacent station was opened by the Charing Cross & Hampstead
   Railway as OXFORD STREET on 22 June 1907
Name of this adjacent station renamed TOTTENHAM COURT ROAD on
   9 March 1908
The first Tottenham Court Road station was then (9 March 1908) renamed
   Goodge Street

Although 'Tottenham' appears in both Tottenham Court Road and
Tottenham Hale, it is thought that they may be derived from the names of
two separate Old Saxon chiefs both known by the name Totta. 'Tottenham
Hale' means 'Totta's corner of land' (from the Old English *healh*, 'a corner
of land'), and 'Tottenham' means 'Totta's village'. As the names were so
similar, they eventually became identical in form. If Tottenham had not
existed, it is probable that Tottenham Hale would have become Totnal –
but Tottenham was the eventual form of the name.

TOTTENHAM HALE N17
Victoria   (see TOTTENHAM COURT ROAD)
Opened on 1 September 1968

TOTTERIDGE (TOTTERIDGE & WHETSTONE) HERTFORDSHIRE
Northern
Opened by the Great Northern Railway as TOTTERIDGE on 1 April 1872
Name changed to TOTTERIDGE & WHETSTONE on 1 April 1874
First used by Underground trains on 14 April 1940

'Totta's ridge' – referring to a Saxon settler there. (See
also WHETSTONE)

TOWER GATEWAY EC3
Docklands (Bank Branch)
Opened on 31 August 1987

This is situated near Tower Bridge Approach, so it is a 'gateway' to this important bridge.

Although Tower Bridge is one of the most memorable landmarks in London, it is only just over a century old. It was opened in 1894 by Edward, Prince of Wales, son of Queen Victoria and later King Edward VII (reigned 1901–10).

TOWER HILL EC2
District, Circle
Opened as MARK LANE on 6 October 1884
Name changed to TOWER HILL on 1 September 1946
Re-sited on 5 February 1967

The road Tower Hill, running beside the Tower of London, has the dubious distinction of having been one of the principal places of execution in London. Famous victims include Sir Thomas More, Thomas Cromwell, the Duke of Somerset, John Dudley, the Earl of Strafford, Archbishop Laud and the Duke of Monmouth.

The last executions took place there as late as 1780, and there is a stone in Trinity Square to indicate the exact spot where the executions took place.

The name Tower Hill is self-explanatory. The Tower of London itself was begun by William the Conqueror (reigned 1066–87) and has been at the centre of English history ever since – even holding important enemy prisoners during the Second World War.

Within walking distance: All Hallows-by-the-Tower
Design Museum
HMS *Belfast*
London Wall
St Katharine Docks
St Olave
Tower Bridge
Tower Hill Scaffold Memorial
The Tower of London

TUFNELL PARK N7
Northern
Opened on 22 June 1907

Named after the owner of the land in the mid-eighteenth century, William Tufnell. He was a brewer's son who had the luck to become rich by inheriting money from wealthy relations, and so became the lord of the manor of Barnsbury. He inherited this estate from his godfather on condition that he changed his name to Joliffe – so he called himself William Tufnell Joliffe to comply with this somewhat curious request.

Tradition has it that Tufnell Park Road is in fact an old Roman road.

TURNHAM GREEN W4
District, Piccadilly
Opened by the London & South Western Railway on 1 January 1869
First used by Underground trains on 1 June 1877
Rebuilt station opened on 3 December 1911

'Green place near the village of Turnham'. The 'ham' element means either a 'homestead' or else 'riverside pasture' and 'turn' refers to 'the land within a bend in a river'.

THE BATTLE OF TURNHAM GREEN

Turnham Green is a peaceful enough suburban area today – but it witnessed a crucial moment in the Civil War, when the Royalist forces, commanded by King Charles I were intercepted by the Parliamentarian army under the command of the Earl of Essex.

The battle took place in November 1642, three weeks after the Battle of Edgehill, in which the Royalists had won a narrow victory. The king withdrew to Oxford, where he made the mistake of delaying too long before marching south to take London. The delay led to disaster. When he did turn towards London, the Parliamentarians were ready to meet him in force, and the encounter at Turnham Green was an unequal one, with the Parliamentarians having an army of about 24,000 men and the Royalists having between 7,000 and 12,000.

It was more of a standoff than a battle. Charles decided not to engage his troops in a major battle and withdrew, retreating back to Oxford. Only a few shots were made, and there were hardly any casualties or losses. Yet the encounter – not worth the name of a battle – was a crucial factor in Charles's ultimate defeat, because he could not win the war without capturing London – and the opportunity such as he might have had at Turnham Green, never came to him again.

Think of poor King Charles I as you travel into London from Turnham Green on the District or Piccadilly Line.

TURNPIKE LANE N8
Piccadilly
Opened on 19 September 1932

'Lane beside a toll-gate'. Turnpike gates gained their name because they were constructed with large vertical spikes – thus making it difficult or impossible for horses to jump over them.

A TOLLGATE STILL IN USE!

The last major turnpike in England was that at Mile End Road, which was pulled down as late as 1866. However, quite astonishingly, a tollgate is still functioning in the twenty-first century in the College Road, Dulwich.

The original tollgate was constructed in 1789 by John Morgan, who built a road from the top of the hill down to some fields that he rented from Dulwich College. After his death, the College continued to charge people – and animals – to pass through their property. In 1983 the charge for cars was 5p, but in 2005 this had gone up to 50p.

UPMINSTER ESSEX
District
Opened by the London, Tilbury & Southend Railway on 1 May 1885
First used by Underground trains on 2 June 1902

'Upminster' means 'a large church on rising ground' or 'upper church'. In this case, the present Church of St Lawrence goes back to the eleventh or twelfth century, but there may have been a church here previously at Chafford (the original name) as early as the seventh century.

UPMINSTER BRIDGE ESSEX
District   (see UPMINSTER)
Opened on 17 December 1934

This station gets its name because it is situated near a small iron road bridge called Upminster Bridge, over the little river Ingrebourne.

UPNEY ESSEX
District
Opened on 12 September 1932

'Upney' means 'up on an island' – indicating that it is slightly higher and drier land which is raised above the surrounding marshes.

UPTON PARK E7
District, Hammersmith & City
Opened by the London, Tilbury & Southend Railway in 1877
First used by Underground trains on 2 June 1902

'The upper estate'. Over the years the manor of this estate has had various names: first as Rooke Hall then as Upton House and then Ham House.

UXBRIDGE MIDDLESEX
Metropolitan, Piccadilly
Opened on 4 July 1904
Re-sited on 4 December 1938

A Saxon family called the Wixan are believed to have built themselves a bridge across the Colne river here, so this became known as the Wyxebrigge, or Wixan-bridge.

VAUXHALL SW8
Victoria
Opened on 23 July 1971

The origin of the name Vauxhall goes back to the reign of King John (reigned 1199–1216), when the Norman baron Falkes de Breauté, built himself a house here. It became known as Fulke's Hall. There were many variant spellings, such as Faukeshall, or Foxhall – but eventually it settled into 'Vauxhall', which has remained.

What we now call Vauxhall Bridge, which opened in 1816, was originally called Regent's Bridge after the Prince of Wales, who later became George IV (reigned 1820–30), but who was at that time acting as Regent for his father, George III.

Within walking distance: Tate Britain

The old village of Vauxhall in 1825.

The 'Italian Walk' in the once-famous Vauxhall pleasure gardens.

VICTORIA SW1
Circle, District, Victoria
Opened on 24 December 1868

Named after Queen Victoria, whose reign (1837–1901) was the longest of all British monarchs.

Victoria Street, which leads to Victoria Station, was opened in 1851, cutting through what were then the slums of Westminster, and providing a vista of Westminster Abbey and the then newly built Houses of Parliament.

The main-line terminus, Victoria Station, was opened in 1860 at the west end of Victoria Street. The station took its name from the street, and subsequently the whole area came to be known simply as 'Victoria'.

Within walking distance: Buckingham Palace
                            Queen's Gallery
                            Royal Mews
                            Westminster Cathedral

WALTHAMSTOW CENTRAL E17
Victoria
Opened as WALTHAMSTOW (HOE STREET) by the Great Eastern Railway
*   on 26 April 1870*
Name changed to WALTHAMSTOW CENTRAL on 6 May 1868
First used by Underground trains on 1 September 1968

'Walthamstow' means holy place (*stow*) of the Abbess Wilcume. Wilcume was an abbess who lived here some time before the Norman Conquest. In 1067 its name is recorded as Wilcumestuue.

WANSTEAD E11
Central
Opened on 14 December 1947

'Homestead by a small hill'. Alternatively the 'wan' part may refer to a wagon or *wain* – as in John Constable's painting, *The Haywain*. Unfortunately, the exact meaning of this name is not clear.

WAPPING E1
East London Line
Opened by the East London Railway as WAPPING & SHADWELL on
*   7 December 1869*
Name changed to WAPPING on 10 April 1876
First used by Underground trains on 1 October 1884
After much rebuilding, Second World War bombing and subsequent
*   rebuilding, station was finally finished in 1982*

Like almost all names ending in 'ing', Wapping tells us that a Saxon leader, probably called something like Waeppa, settled here with his family and followers. 'Wapping' means 'place where Waeppa's people live'.

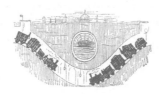

WARREN STREET W1
Northern, Victoria
Opened as EUSTON ROAD on 22 June 1907
Name changed to WARREN STREET on 7 June 1908

Warren Street, built in 1790–91, is named after Sir Peter Warren, a well-known and important eighteenth-century vice-admiral. Few people remember him now, but he has a monument in Westminster Abbey. His son-in-law, Charles Fitzroy, 1st Baron Southampton, owned the land, and named the street after his wife, Anne Warren, and his famous father-in-law, Sir Peter. The Underground station is named after the street.

WARWICK AVENUE W2
Bakerloo
Opened on 31 January 1915

Warwick Avenue is named after Jane Warwick, an heiress who married Sir John Morshead. Her family once lived in this area, in Paddington Manor.

WATERLOO SE1
Bakerloo, Northern, Waterloo & City, Jubilee
Waterloo & City Line opened on 8 August 1898
Bakerloo Line opened on 10 March 1906
Northern Line opened on 13 August 1926

The name 'Waterloo' commemorates the historic battle of 1815 in which Napoleon was finally defeated.

At the time of the battle a new bridge was being constructed across the Thames at the western end of the Strand. It was begun in 1811 and was to have been called the Strand Bridge. However, after Wellington's great victory, an Act of Parliament changed its name to Waterloo 'in remembrance of great and glorious achievements'.

The Prince Regent opened the bridge on 18 of June 1817 – the second anniversary of the battle. Inevitably, the new southern approach road was given the name Waterloo Road.

Trains had not been invented at that time, but thirty years later, in 1848, the new railway station built nearby naturally assumed the name 'Waterloo'.

The present bridge over the Thames is a replacement of the original, which began to show signs of collapse in 1923. The present bridge was constructed between 1937 and 1942.

Within walking distance: London Eye
                                  London Aquarium
                                  Houses of Parliament and Big Ben
                                  Tate Britain
                                  Westminster Abbey
                                  Whitehall

WATFORD HERTFORDSHIRE
Metropolitan
Opened on 2 November 1925

'Watford' means 'the hunter's ford' – deriving from the Old English word *wath*, meaning 'hunting'. The ford in this case crosses the river Colne.

WEMBLEY CENTRAL MIDDLESEX
Bakerloo
Opened by the London & Birmingham Railway as SUDBURY in 1842
Name changed to SUDBURY & WEMBLEY on 1 May 1882
Name changed again to WEMBLEY FOR SUDBURY on 1 November 1910
First used by Underground trains on 16 April 1917
Name finally changed to WEMBLEY CENTRAL on 5 July 1948

In the ninth century this area was referred to as *Wemba Lea*, or 'the meadows where Wemba lived'. Wemba was another long-forgotten Saxon chieftain.

WEMBLEY PARK MIDDLESEX
Jubilee, Metropolitan   (see WEMBLEY CENTRAL)
Opened on 12 May 1894

The site of the original 'Park' is now taken by Wembley Stadium exhibition and entertainment centre.

WEST ACTON W3
Central   (see ACTON)
Opened on 5 November 1923

WESTBOURNE PARK W2
Hammersmith & City
Opened on 1 February 1866

'Westbourne' derives from the two Saxon words, *westan*, 'west', and *burnam*, 'place', and was evidently referring to a 'place west of …' something. The 'something' was in fact a little stream, which took its name from the district, becoming known as the Westbourne. In other words, the area gave the name to the stream – rather than vice versa. There used to be a Westbourne Farm here, and in much earlier times the river was called Knightsbridge Brook, or Bayswater Rivulet.

Westbourne Park, Westbourne Grove, Westbourne Terrace: all these and other 'Westbourne' places are associated with this early beginning.

No one ever sees the river Westbourne nowadays, but its waters are still here, dammed up and forming the Serpentine in Hyde Park. It was the idea of Queen Caroline, the wife of George II (reigned 1727–60) to create the Serpentine in 1730.

The word 'serpentine' means 'like a snake' and refers to the gently winding contours of its design. It was the height of fashion in those years to make lakes and paths 'serpentine' in contrast to the French preference for geometrical patterns and straight lines, as in the gardens of Versailles.

Nowadays the Westbourne river leaves the Serpentine in the Ranalagh Sewer on its way to the Thames. In former years, the bridge across it gave us the name of Knightsbridge. (See KNIGHTSBRIDGE)

WEST BROMPTON SW10
District
Opened on 12 April 1869

'Western part of the farm or area where broom grows'.

WESTFERRY E14
Docklands
Opened on 31 August 1987

There are several 'Westferry' names in this area, reminding us of the ferries which were once so necessary to cross the Thames. West Ferry Road was once known as the Deptford and Greenwich Ferry Road.

Although the ferries are no longer here, the name of this Docklands station is now a memorial to them like Horseferry Road near the Houses of Parliament, which led down to the Thames to ferry horses across to Lambeth.

WEST FINCHLEY N12
Northern   (see FINCHLEY CENTRAL)
Opened by the London & North Eastern Railway on 1 March 1933
First used by Underground trains on 14 April 1940

WEST HAM E7
District, Hammersmith & City, Jubilee
(see EAST HAM)
Opened by the London Tilbury & Southend Railway on 1 February 1901
First used by Underground trains on 2 June 1902

'Western part of the riverside pasture'.

WEST HAMPSTEAD NW6
Jubilee   (see HAMPSTEAD)
Opened on 30 June 1879

WEST HARROW MIDDLESEX
Metropolitan   (see HARROW-ON-THE-HILL)
Opened on 17 November 1913

WEST INDIA QUAY E14
Docklands
Opened on 31 August 1987

Named after the West India Docks, which opened in 1802 and
closed in 1980. These docks were originally built for trade with the
West Indies but later used for India and the Far East.

WEST KENSINGTON W14
District   (see KENSINGTON (OLYMPIA))
Opened as NORTH END (FULHAM) on 9 September 1874
Name changed to WEST KENSINGTON on 1 March 1877

WESTMINSTER SW1
Circle, District, Jubilee
Opened as WESTMINSTER BRIDGE on 24 December 1868
Name changed to WESTMINSTER in 1907

It must have been a Londoner who first named Westminster – for it
means 'the monastery in the west'. Its very name implies that it is to
the west of a London that already existed.

Within walking distance: Banqueting House
                                 Cabinet War Rooms
                                 Cenotaph
                                 Downing Street
                                 Horse Guards
                                 Houses of Parliament and Big Ben
                                 London Eye
                                 Royal Festival Hall
                                 St Margaret's
                                 Westminster Abbey
                                 Westminster Cathedral

THE CITY AND PALACE OF WESTMINSTER: LEGACY OF A SAXON KING AND SAINT

It was the Saxon King and Saint, Edward the Confessor (reigned 1042–66) who first began to build a palace at Westminster, when he was rebuilding an ancient monastery here – now known as Westminster Abbey.

Three centuries earlier, King Offa of Mercia (d. 796) had founded a small monastery here on Thorney Island (Isle of Brambles) in the triangle formed where the Tyburn river forked near the present St James's Park Underground Station, reaching the Thames in two separate streams.

Edward the Confessor's decision to settle here and move away from London had an immensely profound effect on London's history, separating the seat of government at Westminster from the centre of commercial activity in the City of London.

Visitors to London do not always realise that Westminster and London are two separate cities. The boundaries as you pass (almost imperceptibly) from one to the other are marked by statues of griffins – the unofficial badge of the City of London.

Strictly speaking, these are dragons, but are usually referred to as 'griffins'.

Perhaps the easiest one to find is in the middle of the road marking where Temple Bar used to be, as the Strand leads into Fleet Street. There is another on the pavement almost opposite Cleopatra's Needle on the north side of the road. (See also the entry on WESTMINSTER ABBEY on page 162)

WEST RUISLIP MIDDLESEX
Central   (see RUISLIP)

The main-line station was opened as RUISLIP & ICKENHAM by the Great Western & Great Central Joint Committee on 2 April 1906

Name changed to WEST RUISLIP on 30 June 1947

Underground station opened on 21 November 1948

WEST SILVERTOWN E16
Docklands
Opened on 2 December 2005

'Silvertown' is named after the rubber and telegraph works of S.W. Silver and Co., who had their factory here in the mid-nineteenth century. As it developed, this area took on the name of this large firm.

THE SILVERTOWN EXPLOSION

The area around West Silvertown Docklands Station, now situated in a rapidly developing part of London, was the scene of a terrifying explosion in January 1917, during the First World War. It was the largest single explosion to have taken place in Britain at that time.

To help the war effort, a munitions factory had been set up here – dangerously, in the middle of a highly populated area – to produce the chemical explosive Trinitrotoluene (TNT). Safety standards were not strict, and a fatal fire started, which ignited 50 tons of TNT, killing 73 people and injuring over 400. The blast was so great that it is said to have been heard 100 miles away – even at Sandringham in Norfolk. Seventy thousand properties were damaged and thousands of people were left homeless.

Casualty numbers could have been far higher, but fortuitously the explosion happened on a Friday evening when few workers were present on the factory site. Nevertheless the cost to the surrounding buildings was estimated at £2.5 million.

The event is now in memory only, but inside the entrance to the factory location on North Woolwich Road there is a memorial to those who lost their lives in the First and Second World Wars – and in the Silvertown Explosion.

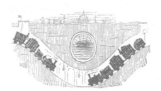

WHITECHAPEL E1
District, Hammersmith & City, East London Line
Opened by the East London Railway on 10 April 1876

Built around 1250, a chapel dedicated to St Mary was built here in white stone. The road to this chapel became known as Whitechapel Road and the whole area has been named from the original chapel, rebuilt three times over the centuries but finally destroyed in 1952.

WHITE CITY W12
Central
Opened by the Hammersmith & City Line as WOOD LANE on
*   1 May 1908*
Opened by the Central Line as WOOD LANE on 14 May 1908
Name changed to WHITE CITY and Central Line and re-sited on
*   23 November 1947*
Hammersmith & City Line closed on 25 October 1959

In 1908, 140 acres were taken here for the Franco-British Exhibition, which was the largest exhibition that had been held in Britain up to that date. Forty acres of gleaming white buildings gave this exhibition centre its name. The 4th Olympic games took place here in the same year.

The centre was commandeered by the government during the First World War and then left derelict afterwards until 1927, when greyhound racing was introduced. The stadium was demolished in 1985 to make way for the BBC White City building.

WILLESDEN GREEN NW10
Jubilee
Opened on 24 November 1879

'Hill with a well or spring' – deriving from the Old English *weill*, 'a spring', and *dun*, 'a hill'.

WILLESDEN JUNCTION NW10
Bakerloo
Opened by the London & North Western Railway on 1 September 1866
First used by Underground trains on 10 May 1915

Named because of the railway junction here.

WIMBLEDON SW19
District
Opened by the London & Southampton Railway on 21 May 1838
First used by Underground trains on 3 June 1889

The *dun*, or 'hill', of a Saxon settler called Winebeald or some similar name.

WIMBLEDON PARK SW19
District   (see WIMBLEDON)
Opened by the London and South Western Railway on 3 June 1889

WOODFORD ESSEX
Central
Opened by the Eastern Counties Railway on 22 August 1856
First used by Underground trains on 14 December 1947

The obvious meaning is that this is a place where there existed a ford in a wooded area. The original ford must have been replaced by a bridge some time in the thirteenth century, for it is referred to as *Wudeforde* in 1225 but *Ponte de Woodford* ('Bridge of Woodford') by 1285. By 1429 it was known as *Woodfordbrigge*.

The ford was situated at the point where a Roman road out of London had to cross the river Roding.

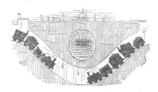

WOOD GREEN N22
Piccadilly
Opened on 19 September 1932

The original hamlet here was situated at a 'green place near the wood'.
Here, the wood referred to is Enfield Chase.

WOOD LANE W12
Hammersmith & City
Opened 12 October 2008

Three stations here have been either replaced, renamed or
demolished – the first one opening 1 May 1908. The present
station, opened in 2008, is a splendid new creation serving the area
and especially useful for access to the Westfield London retail and
leisure centre.

Wood Lane is a self-explanatory and truly rural name dating back
to the early nineteenth century or even earlier. Clearly it tells us of
a time when this was a wooded area with a path running through it.
In no way can this name be applicable to the area in this twenty-first
century, but nevertheless Wood Lane has a thoroughly comfortable
and traditional feel to it, despite its anachronism.

WOODSIDE PARK N12
Northern
Opened by the Great Northern Railway as TORRINGTON PARK on
* 1 April 1872*
Name changed to WOODSIDE PARK on 1 May 1882
First used by Underground trains on 14 April 1940

'Park beside a wood' – in this case the wood referred to is Finchley
Wood. (See FINCHLEY)

WOOLWICH ARSENAL SE18
Docklands (see ARSENAL)
Opened on 10 January 2009

According to Boris Johnson, who opened the station in his capacity as Mayor of London: 'People in this part of London will now be just a 24-minute hop, skip and a jump away from the Olympic site.'

SADLY...

... Charles Pearson, the man who in 1845 had first proposed the construction of a London underground railway, and who had worked so hard to make it possible, died just four months before the first journey was made on 10 January 1863. He never lived to see the results of his hard work and far-sighted imagination.

The Fairlop Oak – the gigantic ancient tree that gave its name to Fairlop. (see FAIRLOP, page 50.)

CAPITAL WORDS

A Selection of Famous London Names

ALBERT HALL SW7

Everyone knows that this great hall is named after Prince Albert, the consort of Queen Victoria. He died in 1861, aged forty-one, and Victoria spent the remaining forty years of her life in perpetual mourning for him. Ten years earlier, in 1851, Prince Albert had organised The Great Exhibition, and the cluster of museums in South Kensington and the Albert Hall itself were paid for out of the profits of that event.

What is less well known is that Queen Victoria herself named the hall – startling spectators at the ceremony for the laying of the foundation stone by suddenly announcing the name it was to bear.

Originally, it was to be known simply as The Hall of Arts and Sciences – but as she laid the foundation stone the Queen surprised the assembly by declaring that 'Royal Albert' would be added to the proposed name. Today no one uses the phrase 'Arts and Sciences' in its name – it has become, simply, the Royal Albert Hall.

Nearest Underground station:
South Kensington   *Circle, District, Piccadilly*

BERKELEY SQUARE W1

Named after Lord Berkeley of Stratton (d. 1678), who was an
ambassador to Sweden and a vigorous commander of part of the
Royalist forces during the Civil War. After the Restoration in 1660
he had a palatial mansion built in this area, which is no longer in
existence. His name, however, lives on in Berkeley Square, Berkeley
Street and the Berkeley Hotel.

Nearest Underground station:
Green Park   *Jubilee, Piccadilly, Victoria*

BIRDCAGE WALK SW1

This road, along the south side of St James's Park, is on the site of
James I's Royal Menagerie and Aviary, which was enlarged later by
Charles II. There were many cages of rare birds there. In 1661 Samuel
Pepys wrote in his diary that he walked 'in St James's Park, and saw
great variety of fowl which I never saw before'.

A few years later, in 1665, John Evelyn described his own visit
there: '… I saw various animals, and examined the throat of ye
"Onocratylus", or Pelican, a fowle between a Stork and a Swan,
a melancholy waterfowl brought from Astracan by the Russian
Ambassador; it was diverting to see how he would toss up and turn a
flat fish, plaice or flounder, to get it right into its gullet…'

Although the cages are no longer there, St James's Park is still the
home of many interesting species of bird.

Nearest Underground stations:
Westminster   *Circle, District*
St James's Park   *Circle, District*

BUCKINGHAM PALACE

Named after John Sheffield (1648–1721) who was Lord Chamberlain
to James II and a cabinet councillor under William III. Queen
Anne created him Duke of Buckingham in 1703. He was a man of
importance during these reigns, and as well as being prominent in
politics, he was also a poet and playwright and a friend of John Dryden
and Alexander Pope. However, on the death of Queen Anne he fell
out of favour and intrigued to bring the Stuarts back to the throne.

Nowadays, he is little remembered, but his name is perpetuated due to the fact that in 1702–05 he built a grand house for himself, called Buckingham House, on the site of what is now Buckingham Palace.

George III bought Buckingham House in 1762, and it became known as The Queen's House. Then, when George IV (reigned 1820–30) came to the throne, he enlarged the house to such an extent that it became Buckingham Palace. He never lived in it himself, and it was left to his niece Queen Victoria (reigned 1837–1901) to be the first monarch to take up residence there.

Nearest Underground stations:
St James's Park   *Circle, District*
Victoria   *Circle, District, Victoria*

BURLINGTON HOUSE, PICCADILLY W1

Burlington House is famed today for its major art exhibitions, visitors to which have the added pleasure of visiting the last remaining example of the great mansions built by wealthy noblemen in the Piccadilly area shortly after the Restoration in 1660.

It is named after Richard Boyle, 1st Earl of Burlington (1612–97), a statesman who supported the Royalists during the Civil War and was an active politician supporting William and Mary at the time of the 'Glorious Revolution' of 1688.

Nearest Underground station:
Piccadilly   *Bakerloo, Victoria*

CARNABY STREET W1

Famous, especially in the '60s, for its colourful clothing shops for the trendy hippie generation – even entering the Oxford English Dictionary to mean 'fashionable clothing for young people'. In 1683, Richard Tyler, a bricklayer and developer, built himself a house in this road, which he named Karnaby House – but no one knows why. The street is named after this.

Nearest Underground station:
Oxford Circus   *Bakerloo, Central, Victoria*

CENOTAPH SW1

The Cenotaph in Whitehall is so much a part of the London scene that its somewhat curious name is rarely questioned. It means 'empty tomb' from the two Greek words *kenos*, 'empty' and *taphos*, 'tomb'.

Designed in 1919 by Sir Edwin Lutyens to commemorate those killed in the First World War, it has an interesting shape – although it looks geometrically regular, in fact there is no single straight line in its design. If you were to continue the almost imperceptible curves of the sides, they would meet at a point about 1,000 feet (304.8 metres) from their starting points.

Unlike the Tomb of the Unknown Warrior, it contains no body and there is no religious symbolism. It is decorated simply with the flags of the three services and the Merchant Navy.

Nearest Underground station:
Westminster   *Circle, District, Jubilee*

CLARENCE HOUSE SW1

Clarence House has been the home of many members of the Royal Family since it was completed in 1828. It was built for William, Duke of Clarence and heir to the throne, who became William IV in 1830 on the death of his brother, George IV.

George IV had greatly transformed and enlarged Buckingham House into Buckingham Palace, to make it fit for British monarchs – but he did not live to occupy it himself. William hated it and proposed it should be turned into a new Houses of Parliament when the old building was burnt down in 1834. Instead, William continued to live at his own 'Clarence House' – the name by which it has always been called.

Nearest Underground stations:
Green Park   *Jubilee, Piccadilly, Victoria*
St James's Park   *Circle, District*

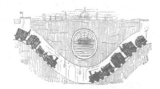

'COCKNEY'

The word 'cockney' is known worldwide as a name given to Londoners and 'cockney rhyming slang' as the extraordinary and unique vocabulary that they often use.

The strange origin of 'cockney' goes back to the Middle Ages when country people used the word to refer to people who lived in towns. It was a term of contempt, deriving from *cockeney*, or 'cock's egg' – a small, misshapen, deformed egg supposedly laid by a cockerel. The point was that town people were no good for anything, as they were considered ignorant of country skills and, perhaps, as living 'softer' lives.

Eventually, the word has come to refer exclusively to Londoners – especially those who are born within the sound of 'Bow Bells', that is, the bells of St Mary-le-Bow in Cheapside. This church was destroyed by bombs in 1941 but was re-built 1956–62.

Traditionally, cockneys have a very sharp wit, and are often chirpily disrespectful of authority or members of the 'posh' upper classes who take themselves too seriously.

DUKE OF YORK COLUMN SW1

This somewhat pretentious and unnecessary column is named after Frederick, Duke of York (1763–1827), the second son of George IV. He was made Commander-in-Chief of the British Army from 1798 to 1809, but his military career was rather less than spectacular, as described in the children's nursery rhyme:

> The Grand Old Duke of York,
> He had ten thousand men;
> He marched them all to the top of the hill,
> And marched them down again.

The rhyme refers to an abortive operation led by the Duke against the French forces in Flanders in 1794. To put the record straight, however, the 'old' duke was only twenty-nine at the time, he had 30,000 men, and there was no hill.

The column is 124 feet high (37.8 metres) and was completed in 1833, some years after the Duke's death, and was paid for mainly by stopping one day's pay for every soldier in the army – an imposition that did not endear him, posthumously, to his former troops. They suggested that the height of the column was such as to enable the debt-ridden Duke to keep out of the clutches of his creditors (he owed £2,000,000).

Second sons of British monarchs are traditionally given the title of Duke of York. Notably, New York is named after James, Duke of York (1633–1701), who was the second son of Charles I.

Nearest Underground station:
St James's Park   *Circle, District*

FLEET STREET EC4

Fleet Street is (or was) synonymous with the world of newspapers, and the term 'Fleet Street' is still used to refer to the 'tittle-tattle' of the press. However, with modern techniques of newspaper production, much of the trade has now departed from Fleet Street itself.

The name itself is taken from the Fleet river – one of the many tributaries flowing into the Thames. In former times these were fair-sized rivers, but they are now 'tamed' and run underground in pipes and sewers.

'Fleet' is derived from the Old English word *fleot*, meaning 'flowing water', and is linked with the modern English words 'float' and 'flood'. It could also mean a 'tidal inlet'. The almost invisible Fleet river rises at Hampstead and flows into the Thames at Blackfriars Bridge.

Nearest Underground station:
Blackfriars   *Circle, District*
Temple   *Circle, District*

GROSVENOR SQUARE W1

Grosvenor Square, Grosvenor Hill, Grosvenor Place, Grosvenor Street, Grosvenor Road: all these names and several more are associated with the enormously wealthy Grosvenor family, who for three centuries have owned vast areas in Mayfair, Belgravia and Pimlico.

The first Grosvenor to become involved in all these London estates was a young Baronet from Cheshire, Sir Thomas Grosvenor, who gained his fortune by marrying a wealthy heiress, Mary Davies – aged only twelve – in St Clement Danes in 1677.

The Grosvenor family name goes back to Norman times, when it must have been something of a nickname: '*le gros veneur*' which means 'the fat huntsman'.

Queen Victoria gave the title Duke of Westminster to Hugh Lupus Grosvenor in 1874. The present Duke, who is the 6th Duke of Westminster, is the 3rd richest person in Great Britain.

Nearest Underground stations:

Bond Street	*Central, Jubilee*
Green Park	*Jubilee, Piccadilly, Victoria*

HAYMARKET SW1

For several centuries, from Tudor times onward, the royal stables were kept on the site now occupied by Trafalgar Square. Horses need hay and straw, so it was convenient to have a thriving hay market nearby.

It was not until 1830 that the last bundle of hay was sold here, when the market itself moved to Cumberland Market, just north of Regent's Park.

Nearest Underground station:

Piccadilly Circus	*Bakerloo, Piccadilly*

HORSEFERRY ROAD SW1

Like the Haymarket, Horseferry Road gained its name by being literally what it says it is.

The road led to what used to be the only horse ferry allowed to ply its trade in, or near, London. The ferry was situated between the present Westminster Bridge, opened in 1750, and Lambeth Bridge, opened a century later in 1861.

The ferry was still in use even in the nineteenth century, and the profitable tolls belonged to the Archbishops of Canterbury, whose palace at Lambeth is situated nearly opposite Horseferry Road on the south bank of the Thames.

Almost unbelievably, London Bridge was the *only* bridge over the Thames until 1750, so when Westminster Bridge was built it was a disaster for the Thames watermen, who for centuries had vigorously opposed the building of any other bridge over the river.

They were given £25,000 in compensation, an enormous sum in those days, and the Archbishop, who owned the ferry, was given £21,025.

Nearest Underground station:
Westminster   *Circle, District, Jubilee*

LORD'S CRICKET GROUND NW8

This world-famous cricket ground has no connection with the House of Lords or any English lord but is in fact named after a London wine merchant, Thomas Lord (1755–1832).

He was passionately keen on cricket, and was encouraged by wealthy friends to establish a new cricket ground for Middlesex Cricket Club. In 1787 he took possession of what was then little more than an open field, 'Mary-le-bone Field', which was used for a variety of sporting activities including pigeon shooting and 'hopping matches'. He moved from this to another field in 1810, but soon found that a part of this was to be used for the new Regent's Canal. Finally, he moved, in 1814, to the present site in St John's Wood Road.

Thomas Lord retired in 1825 after thirty-eight years of association with the MCC – but his name is forever used by the cricketing world whenever a prestigious match is to be played. His portrait by George Morland still hangs in the pavilion at the present-day Lord's.

Nearest Underground station:
Warwick Avenue   *Bakerloo*

THE MALL and PALL MALL SW1

The interesting origin of the name The Mall is that it comes from the Italian word for a game similar to croquet, involving hitting a ball (*palla*) through an iron ring with a mallet (*maglio*).

The game of 'pall mall' was popular in the seventeenth century, and was played in an alley where the present road, Pall Mall, is situated. When this alley was made into a road, a new course for the game was created in about 1660, very shortly after Charles II came to the throne – and this course came to be known as The Mall.

The game lost its popularity in the eighteenth century, and The Mall became a place where it was fashionable for ladies and gentlemen to promenade. It was only after the death of Queen Victoria in 1901 that, in her memory, a 'New Mall' was created as a wide and impressive route from Admiralty Arch to the Queen Victoria Memorial in front of Buckingham Palace.

Nearest Underground station:
St James's Park *Circle, District*

PATERNOSTER ROW and PATERNOSTER SQUARE EC4

Pater noster is, of course, the Latin for 'Our Father' – the beginning of the Lord's Prayer.

According to John Stow (1525–1605), the famous London historian who wrote his great *Survey of London and Westminster* in 1598, Paternoster Row gained its name because in medieval times bead makers lived in this road, making rosaries. The prayers recited with the use of these rosaries prompted the name Paternoster.

Stow may be right in thinking this – but an alternative explanation may simply be that the clergy of St Paul's could often have been heard praying aloud in the neighbourhood of their cathedral, which lay nearby.

Nearest Underground station:
St Paul's *Central*

PETTICOAT LANE E1

This Sunday street market near Liverpool Street Station is officially called Middlesex Street, but such is its huge popularity that the traditional name, Petticoat Lane, has never been allowed to be forgotten. In the Middle Ages it was called Hog's Lane, but this had changed to Petticoat Lane by the end of the seventeenth century – named for the selling of old clothes there. But, as everyone knows, there is an enormous range of goods on sale here today, with stalls spreading all around the neighbouring area.

Nearest Underground station:
Aldgate *Circle, Metropolitan*

PORTOBELLO ROAD W11

It may seem far-fetched to say that Christopher Columbus named Portobello Road, but in fact the history of this foreign sounding word shows that he did – although admittedly in an indirect way.

When Columbus discovered a small bay in Panama, Central America, he admired it so much that he called it 'Porto Bello' – beautiful port. The Spanish founded a town here in 1597 and developed it as a port, but its strategic and commercial importance led to constant attacks by the British.

The English naval commander Admiral Vernon (1684–1757) captured Porto Bello from the Spanish in 1739 – a victory which was greeted with great delight in Britain, leading to a number of places being re-named Portobello, including a farm in this area – which was then open countryside north of London.

In the eighteenth century, the road we know today as Portobello Road was just a farm track leading to this Porto Bello Farm. Then, in the nineteenth century, the Saturday street market started to become popular, at first as a centre for horse dealing.

Nearest Underground station:
Ladbroke Grove   *Hammersmith & City*

HAVE YOU EVER FELT 'GROGGY'?

The eighteenth-century British admiral mentioned above – Edward Vernon – became known as 'Old Grog' because of the coat of 'grogram' that he wore – a coarse-grained cloth which derived its name from the French *gros grain*, or 'coarse thread'.

He was the much-feared naval Commander-in-Chief West Indies, who in 1740 ordered watered-down rum to be served to both officers and men. Naturally, this made him very unpopular and the mixture itself was nicknamed 'grog'.

If you take too much 'grog' or more generally nowadays if you are feeling unsteady or unwell, you say you are feeling 'groggy'. So, whenever you do feel groggy – spare a thought for Admiral Vernon, the celebrated man who captured Porto Bello.

PUDDING LANE EC3

The Great Fire of London started in this lane, in Farryner's bakery, on 2 September 1666. The Monument was built to commemorate this crucial event in London's history. (See MONUMENT on page 85)

Alas, this 'lane' is now the scene of massive modern buildings and is totally different from the picturesque place you might hope to see, judging from its name.

The name itself, Pudding Lane, is perhaps deceptive, probably conjuring up images of delicious sweet desserts. However, the original meaning of 'pudding' was 'guts' and 'entrails'. Pudding Lane almost certainly got its name from filthy droppings from carts taking unwanted offal from the butchers in Eastcheap down to the river Thames.

This original meaning of 'pudding' is perpetuated in the dish known as 'black pudding' – made largely with blood.

Nearest Underground station:
Monument   *Circle, District*

RITZ HOTEL W1

Opened in 1906, the Ritz Hotel is named after its first owner, César Ritz (1850–1918), who built its exterior to resemble the Rue de Rivoli in Paris.

César Ritz was the thirteenth child of a poor Swiss Alpine shepherd. Very few people have been so successful in moving from rags to riches as Monsieur Ritz – in fact his very name has passed into the English language as 'ritzy', meaning glitteringly and ostentatiously smart and luxurious.

Nearest Underground station:
Piccadilly   *Bakerloo, Piccadilly*

ROTTEN ROW SW7

Rotten Row is a sandy track almost a mile in length, which runs along the south side of Hyde Park adjacent to South Carriage Drive. It was laid out by William III (reigned 1689–1702) as a route through Hyde Park along which to ride between St James's Palace and Kensington Palace, where he had set up his court.

It was known as the *Route du Roi* – the 'King's Road' – and, over time, people used the name 'Rotten Row' as a garbled version of this French phrase.

It is still used by the Household Cavalry, who exercise their horses here – and members of the public may also use it for riding lessons and practice.

William III needed to feel safe at night as he travelled along this track – so he had it lit with 300 oil lamps in 1690 – the first artificially lit highway in Britain.

Nearest Underground station:
Knightsbridge   *Piccadilly*

SADLER'S WELLS E1

In the Middle Ages the Priory of St John's at Clerkenwell had a holy well here, but this was covered over at the time of the Reformation and became quite forgotten.

In 1683 the owner of the land, a Mr Thomas Sadler, re-discovered the well, and the waters were considered to be so health-giving that for a while the well made a good profit as a medicinal spa. As a side attraction, Thomas Sadler built a 'musick house' here.

Since this time, music, pantomime and dance have been features of the succession of theatres built here on the site of Mr Sadler's original popular well – which can still be seen under a trap door at the back of the present theatre's stalls.

Nearest Underground station:
Angel   *Northern Line City Branch*

ST BARTHOLOMEW'S HOSPITAL EC1

St Bartholomew's – popularly known as 'Bart's' – is the oldest hospital in London, founded in 1123, but why it was founded and how its got its name belongs, literally, to the world of dreams.

According to tradition, Rahere, a courtier of Henry I (reigned 1100–45) had gone on a pilgrimage to Rome and had suffered a fever on his way there. He made a vow that if he recovered he would build a hospital in London when he got back home. The legend tells how St Bartholomew appeared to Rahere in a dream and said:

'I have chosen a place in a suburb of London at Smoothfield where, in my name, thou shalt found a church.'

The prediction came true. When Rahere did return, Henry I granted him a strip of land just outside the city wall, at Smithfield ('Smoothfield') and this was where he built a hospital and a priory.

Rahere's vow has now helped the sick for almost 1,000 years. Among its patients was Wat Tyler, who was taken there after he was stabbed by the Lord Mayor of London during the Peasants' Revolt in 1381.

Nearest Underground stations:

Barbican	*Circle, Hammersmith & City, Metropolitan*
Blackfriars	*Circle, District*
Farringdon	*Circle, Hammersmith & City, Metropolitan*
St Paul's	*Central*

SAVILE ROW W1

Named after Lady Dorothy Savile, the wife of the 3rd Earl of Burlington. Today the street is associated with fine tailoring, but it was a fashionable residential street in the eighteenth century, when it was originally laid out.

Richard Sheridan the dramatist (1751–1816) lived and died here at No. 14.

Nearest Underground station:

Oxford Circus	*Bakerloo, Central, Victoria*

SAVOY HOTEL WC2

The Savoy Hotel, famous as one of London's most luxurious hotels, is built on land on which the former Savoy Palace stood. This belonged to Peter, Count of Savoy and uncle to Queen Eleanor of Provence, the French wife of Henry III (reigned 1216–72).

Henry III gave the palace to Peter of Savoy for an annual rental of three barbed arrows. It was one of many enormous medieval palaces built along the banks of the Thames. It had a long and fascinating history: John of Gaunt owned it in the fourteenth century and Geoffrey Chaucer was married in its chapel. In 1510 it became a hospital for the poor.

The Savoy Hotel opened in 1889, with César Ritz as its first manager (see RITZ HOTEL) and Auguste Escoffier as its first chef. It was one of the first London hotels to have electric light and electric lifts. It also had a high ratio of bathrooms to bedrooms – a novel level of hygiene in those days!

Nearest Underground station:
Embankment   *Bakerloo, Circle, District, Northern*

SCOTLAND YARD SW1

The phrase 'Scotland Yard' – or even just 'the Yard' is of course synonymous with the Metropolitan Police Force, which now has its headquarters on Broadway and Victoria Street.

Its official name is now New Scotland Yard, which reminds us that its previous premises were in Great Scotland Yard – a part of the complex of buildings of the old Whitehall Palace – the name 'Scotland' has been linked to that location for over 1,000 years.

The Scottish association began when the Saxon King Edgar (reigned 959–75) gave land near the bank of the Thames to Kenneth III of Scotland (reigned 997–1005) so that Scottish kings could build a palace there for their use when in London. The last Scottish sovereign to live there was Margaret, sister of Henry VIII (reigned 1509–47), who came there after her husband James IV of Scotland was killed on Flodden Field in 1513.

Nearest Underground station (to both Great Scotland Yard and New Scotland Yard):
Westminster   *Circle, District, Jubilee*

THE SERPENTINE W2

The artificial lake in Hyde Park known as The Serpentine was created in the 1730s by Queen Caroline, wife of George II (reigned 1727–60). She was a keen gardener, and followed the fashion, then prevalent, of shaping paths and lakes in a winding, tortuous manner. This growing fashion of landscape gardening emphasised the difference between the English 'natural' style and the more formal geometrical lines preferred by the French King Louis XIV in his gardens at Versailles.

The Serpentine lake was formed by damming the river Westbourne – which followed a markedly winding course here like a twisting snake – 'serpent-like' – hence 'Serpentine'.

Nearest Underground stations:

Knightsbridge	*Piccadilly*
Lancaster Gate	*Central*

SOHO W1

Soho, the area famous for its restaurants and vibrant nightlife, derives its name from the hunting-cry 'So Ho' – especially used when a hare has been started. It is the equivalent of 'Tally-ho', the cry used by fox hunters when a fox breaks cover.

Today it's almost impossible to imagine this part of London being farmland and open countryside with fields and woods, but until the seventeenth century this was an area often used for hunting.

One of the first residents here was the Duke of Monmouth (1649–85), the illegitimate son of Charles II, who led the rebellion against his uncle James II in 1685. It is said that at the battle of Sedgemoor the Duke's forces used 'Soho' as a password and a rallying-cry.

Nearest Underground stations:

Oxford Circus	*Bakerloo, Central, Victoria*
Piccadilly Circus	*Bakerloo, Piccadilly*
Oxford Circus	*Central, Northern*

SOMERSET HOUSE WC2

When Henry VIII died in 1547, he was succeeded by his young son Edward, who was only nine years old. Obviously a regent had to be appointed, so before he died Henry appointed Edward's uncle, the Duke of Somerset, to be 'Lord Protector'.

For five years, until his execution in 1552, the Duke of Somerset was virtually king of England, and on taking office one of his first acts was to build himself a large palace on the banks of the Thames – Somerset House.

This Somerset House was the residence of royalty for almost two centuries but when Queen Charlotte decided that she preferred to live in Buckingham House, Somerset House was demolished. If only she had chosen to live here, perhaps present British kings and queens would still be living in that gracious Thames-side palace.

The present Somerset House was built on the site of the old one, designed by William Chambers and completed by others after his death. It has recently been given a complete makeover and now houses art galleries and museums and has become a home for arts and learning, with an ice rink for open-air skating in the main courtyard in the winter.

Nearest Underground stations:

Embankment	*Bakerloo, Circle, District, Northern*
Temple	*Circle, District*
Waterloo	*Bakerloo, Northern, Waterloo & City, Jubilee*

STRAND WC2

The name of this important street, leading from Charing Cross to the Law Courts, reminds us that in previous centuries, before the Victoria Embankment was built, (1864–70) the buildings here had access right down to the edge of the river. In fact, it was originally a bridle path along the bank of the Thames.

The word 'strand', meaning 'landing place', is hardly used nowadays, but we still speak of being 'stranded', which literally means 'to be driven on shore'.

Nearest Underground stations:

Covent Garden	*Piccadilly*
Embankment	*Bakerloo, Circle, District, Northern*

THAMES

Julius Caesar found that the ancient Britons had given this river a name, and he wrote it down as Tamesis. It is believed that this Celtic word simply meant 'river' – or alternatively, perhaps, 'the dark one'.

Whatever the ultimate derivation, the Thames is the second oldest recorded place name in England. The oldest is Kent – recorded as Kantion by the Greek explorer Pytheas in the fourth century BC.

TRAFALGAR SQUARE WC2

Unlike the sites of land battles, the places where naval engagements have taken place are not the haunt of modern tourists. The result of this is that comparatively few people can pinpoint exactly where Cape Trafalgar is.

It is a quirk of fate that the name of this insignificant little promontory on the south coast of Spain – south-east of Cadiz and west-north-west of the Strait of Gibraltar – should now be known throughout the world, associated with Horatio Nelson and the greatest naval victory in English history. And in modern times, Trafalgar Square is also now forever linked with demonstrations, pigeons, Norwegian Christmas trees and boozy New Year celebrations.

The battle took place on 21 October 1805 but it wasn't until 1829–41 that Trafalgar Square, commemorating the event, was laid out, and it wasn't until 1868 that the four bronze lions by Sir Edwin Landseer were put in place.

In the Middle Ages this area was the site of the Royal Mews where the royal hawks were kept and falconers had their lodgings. Among his many other duties, Geoffrey Chaucer held the post of Clerk of Mews. In later centuries the site was used for the royal stables.

The actual name Trafalgar is derived from Arabic, and may mean 'end of the west' or 'end of the column', which could refer to the Pillars of Hercules.

Nearest Underground station:
Embankment   *Bakerloo, Circle, District, Northern*

WESTMINSTER ABBEY –
AN EXTRAORDINARY
'ROYAL PECULIAR'

It was the Saxon King and Saint, Edward the Confessor (reigned 1042–66) who first began to rebuild an ancient monastery here – now famous throughout the world as Westminster Abbey.

Three centuries earlier, King Offa of Mercia (d. 796) had founded a small monastery here on Thorney Island (Isle of Brambles), in the triangle formed where the Tyburn river forked near the present St James's Park Underground Station, reaching the Thames in two separate streams.

Edward the Confessor's new abbey here was specially built to be the crowning place of English kings – and it is a proud boast that every reigning English monarch has been crowned in Westminster Abbey since 1066. King Harold, defeated by William the Conqueror at the Battle of Hastings in October 1066, had been the first king to be crowned here, just ten months earlier, in the preceding January.

Importantly, Edward the Confessor himself – who for centuries was England's patron saint – is buried here, and throughout the Middle Ages his shrine in Westminster Abbey was considered one of the holiest places in the country, attracting huge numbers of pilgrims hoping for cures and spiritual blessing.

However, all English abbeys were ruthlessly abolished by Henry VIII in the 1530s, and most of them were severely damaged or destroyed altogether. Westminster Abbey was no exception. The holy shrine of Edward the Confessor was moved and broken up, and the abbot and all of the monks were forced out of office. They surrendered everything to the king at a miserable little ceremony in the Chapter House on 16 January 1540.

For almost a year, the former abbey lay abandoned, but then, in December of that year, Henry VIII decided to 'promote' it into a cathedral with a bishop, dean and prebendaries (canons). So, for almost ten years, Westminster Abbey became Westminster Cathedral, but then, in 1550, under Henry's Protestant son Edward VI, it was absorbed into the diocese of London, so that the Bishop of London had in fact *two* cathedrals.

It was a curious position. But further changes were to take place. When the Catholic Queen Mary came to the throne in 1553, she turned the cathedral back into an abbey complete with new monks, and the shrine of Edward the Confessor was mended and restored to its former importance.

Even then, still further changes were to come – for when the Protestant Queen Elizabeth I came to the throne, the 'abbey' was yet *again* dissolved, on 10 July 1559.

So what exactly is Westminster Abbey today?

Interestingly, Westminster Abbey is one of a very small group of churches known as a 'Royal Peculiar' – in other words it is totally independent of any bishop or even archbishop. It is a free chapel of the Sovereign, and directly under the sole authority of whichever king or queen happens to be on the throne.

Nearest Underground stations:
St James's Park   *Circle, District*
Westminster   *Circle, District, Jubilee*

(For a comment on the word 'Westminster' see WESTMINSTER Underground Station, p.138).

RECOMMENDED FURTHER READING

Ekwall, Eilert, *The Concise Oxford Dictionary of English Place Names*,
    Oxford University Press, 1936
Fairfield, Sheila, *The Streets of London*, Macmillan, 1983
Field, John, *Place-Names of Greater London*, B.T. Batsford Ltd, 1980
Glover, John, *London's Underground*, Ian Allan Publishing, 1996
Halliday, Stephen, *Underground to Everywhere*, Sutton Publishing, 2001
Harris, Cyril M., *What's in a name?*, Capital History, 1977
Leboff, David, *London Underground Stations*, Ian Allan Publishing, 1994
Weinreb, Ben & Christopher Hibbert, *The London Encyclopaedia*,
    Book Club Associates (Macmillan), 1983